GOA

OF SUN 'N SAND

Project Editor: Sadia Dehlvi

Travel Courtesy:
Indian (Formerly, Indian Airlines)

Published 2008 by

Prakash Books India Pvt. Ltd.
1, Ansari Road,Daryaganj
New Delhi 110 002, India.
E-mail: sales@prakashbooks.com
Website: www.prakashbooks.com
Tel: +91-11-23247062-65

ISBN: 978-81-7234-141-1

Printed & bound at: Rave India www.raveindiapress.com

GOA
OF SUN 'N SAND

Text: Valerie Rodrigues

Photographs: Sondeep Shankar
Baud & Eliot Postma

PRAKASH BOOKS

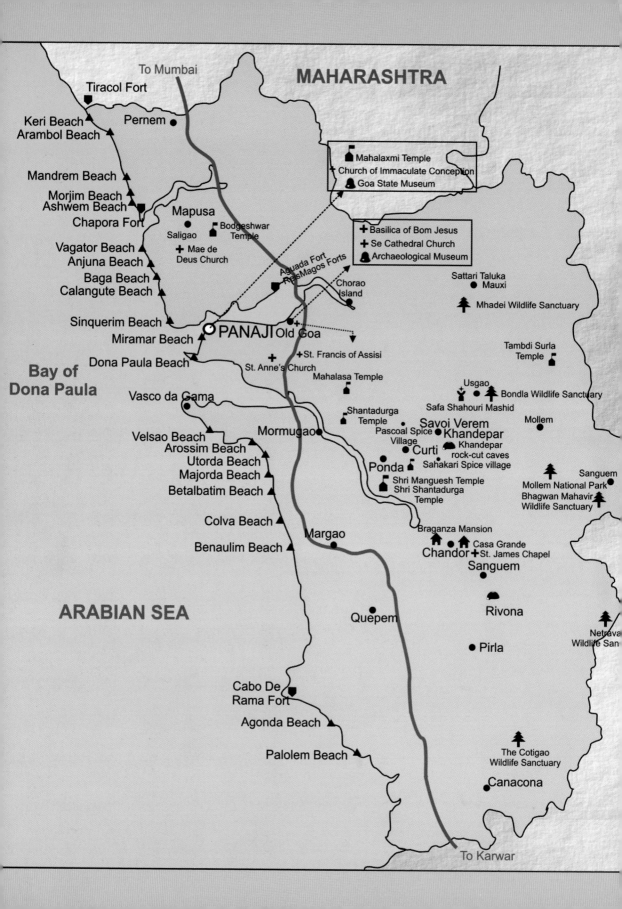

Distances between important places in Goa are given below:-

- Panaji - Bondla: 55 kms.
- Panaji - Calangute: 16 kms.
- Panaji - Cavelossim: 48 kms.
- Panaji - Goa Airport: 29 kms.
- Panaji - Mapusa: 13 kms.
- Panaji - Margao: 33 kms.
- Panaji - Mobor: 50 kms.
- Panaji - Old Goa: 10 kms.
- Panaji - Tiracol: 42 kms.
- Panaj - Vagator: 22 kms.
- Panaji - Varca: 44 kms.
- Panaji - Vasco-da-Gama: 30 kms.
- Margao - Cavelossim: 15 kms.
- Margao - Colva Beach: 6 kms.
- Margao - Goa Airport: 29 kms.
- Margao - Mobor: 17 kms.
- Margao - Varca: 9 kms.
- Vasco-da-Gama - Goa Airport: 3 kms.
- Vasco-da-Gama - Margao: 30 kms.
- Goa Airport - Mobor: 48 kms.
- Dabolim - Varca: 41 kms.

ARNATAKA

LEGEND

- ♠ Houses
- ⚲ Masjid
- ✚ Church
- ▲ Beach
- ● Other Places
- ▼ Forts
- ♠ Wild Life Sanctuary
- ○ State Capital
- ▮ Temple
- ▲ Museum
- ◗ Caves
- ▬ Konkan Railway

Contents

Entering the Flea Market at Anjuna, where you just might manage to pick up a great bargain or two.

Captured.... the colour and good cheer of Carnival.

Travelling Through Time

Right from ancient times, Goa has captured the imagination of all those who visited this beautiful land. From those long-ago centuries, when various dynasties and people fought to gain control of the region, Goa still remains a place that beckons, an enigma that fascinates, a land of eternal charm.

The coastal enchantment of Goa's beautiful sun-kissed beaches and the harmonious blend of Eastern and Western culture are often the first things that attract the casual visitor. But as you explore and start to learn more about Goa, you will find yourself embarking on a journey of rich discovery. You will then begin to understand the real reason why so many people are irresistibly drawn to the place. Goa is endowed not only with beautiful golden beaches, but also with lush green interiors and an incredibly rich cultural heritage. You can swim and surf in the cool blue waters of the sea, hike across the hilly terrain of the forested interiors, visit magnificent churches and temples or wander through old forts and ruins steeped in history. Depending on the season you choose to visit, you can either laze in the sun or watch as the monsoon rains transform the rich red Konkan earth into a lush green paradise. To both the native Goan as well as to the visitor, Goa somehow manages to evoke an intensity of feeling that is difficult to define. Suffice to say that the magic of the land, the warmth and hospitality of her people, and the simple but unique things that characterize the place are enough to captivate and capture the heart.

Panel - A

Panel - B

Legendary Beginnings

There are several charming legends that speak of the origin of Goa. One of the most fascinating tells of how Lord Parashurama, an incarnation of the powerful Hindu god Vishnu, shot an arrow into the Arabian Sea, commanding the waves to part. That hallowed spot where the arrow fell became a new kingdom, a blessed region as it were, the land that is now called Goa. In ancient texts, this land has been referred to by different names like Govarashtra, Goparashtra or Gomant, meaning 'land of cowherds' suggesting that the people who lived here led a simple, nomadic life. Goa was also known as Aparant which translates as 'land beyond the end,' a term used to refer to a place that was perhaps perceived as almost akin to paradise.

Early Rulers

Goa's long and checkered history can be traced back to the 3rd century BC when it was part of the great Mauryan Empire. The discovery of copper plates and other evidence confirms that the Bhoja kings ruled over the land, their capital being at Chandrapur (modern-day Chandor), located in the present Salcete area. Over the next few centuries, historical records indicate that Goa was ruled by a series of ancient Hindu dynasties, including the Chalukyas (of Badami and later of Kalyani), the Rashtrakutas, the Silaharas and the Kadambas. During the reign of the Kadambas, the capital appears to have been shifted to Gopakapattana (now Goa Velha), on the banks of the river Zuari where there was easy access to the sea.

In those days, Goa was a vibrant and thriving centre of sea trade and commerce. Apart from regular exports of rice, arecanut and betel leaves from Goa, ships from lands as distant as Persia, Zanzibar and China sailed back and forth, laden with precious cargo of gold and silver, fine calico and muslin, spices and perfumes. Local industries like spinning, weaving, brass and iron works, oil extraction and shipbuilding flourished. In fact, such was the strength of Goa's currency in its heyday that gold coins embossed with the Kadamba royal crest of a lion and of the patron deity, Saptakoteshwara, were an internationally accepted currency.

The Kadamba dynasty reigned supreme till the mid-thirteenth century when they became feudatory vassals of the Yadavas. In 1312, the Muslim Emperor Alaud-din Khilji sent his army to invade the region under the command of his general Malik Kafur. Gopakapattana was probably razed bare during this invasion, causing the Kadambas to shift their capital back to Chandrapur which, being located on the upper reaches of the river Zuari, was better protected strategically. Around 1327, Mohammed bin Tuglaq attacked the kingdom and destroyed Chandrapur. With the fall of the Goa Kadambas, intermittent plundering continued as the rulers of the Hindu Vijayanagar Empire battled with the Bahamani Muslim Sultanate to gain control of the land. In 1378, Emperor Harihara of the Vijayanagar Empire managed to finally wrest Goa from the Bahamanis. Under the Vijayanagar rule Goa continued to flourish, enjoying a level of wealth and prosperity that became almost legendary. Apart from other precious merchandise, Goa was an important centre for the lucrative trade of the finest horses from Arabia which were much sought-after for the cavalry regiments of the Vijayanagaras and for neighbouring kingdoms in the Deccan.

In 1472, after several intermittent attempts, the Bahamanis mounted another major attack both by land and sea, and managed to wrest back control of the land. Meanwhile, merchant ships were no longer able to easily sail up the river Zuari as it was slowly silting up. The capital was, therefore, shifted further away to Ela on the banks of the river Mandovi, a place the Bahamanis called Gove (present day Old Goa). The Bahamani kingdom fell apart shortly afterwards, splitting into a number of separate sultanates, and Goa was part of the region that fell to Yusuf Adil Shah of Bijapur, in 1489. By this time the riverine port at Ela had become a thriving centre for trade and the town itself was large, with imposing buildings

Above: A statue of the great Maratha king, Chhatrapati Shivaji at Farmagudi, near Ponda.

Left : A portrait of intrepid Portuguese explorer, Vasco da Gama, who landed in India at Calicut in 1498 in search of spices.

Facing page: A depiction of Lord Parashurama at Ancestral Goa (the Big Foot Museum) at Loutolim.

Previous page: Beautiful Portuguese handpainted ceramic tile panels (azulejos) adorn the walls of the Menezes Braganza Institute at Panjim, artistically depicting the adventures of Portuguese explorers. Panel A shows Vasco da Gama at the court of the Zamorin at Calicut. Panel B depicts King Manuel of Portugal on horseback, bidding farewell to the explorer.

धन्य लोहिया धन्य भूमि ही
धन्य तिचे पुत्र
धन्य तयाचा त्याग देखते
जनतेचे नेत्र

DHANYA LOHIA DHANYA BHUMI HI
DHANYA TICHE PUTR
DHANYA TANGELO TYAGA POLLOUPI
BHOUSACHE NETR

MEMORIAL TO THE MARTYRS
OF THE FREEDOM STRUGGLE
AGAINST PORTUGUESE COLONIAL RULE IN INDIA

UNVEILED BY LT. GEN K P CANDETH P. V. S M.
ON 23RD MARCH 1973

ERECTED BY
FREEDOM FIGHTERS ASSOCIATION GOA
THROUGH PUBLIC DONATIONS
DESIGNED BY
ARCHITECT J. R. RALINO DE SOUZA
STRUCTURE BY
ENGINEER AUDHUT KAMAT
AND EXECUTED BY ENGINEER CONTRACTOR S. V. GADGIL

Above: In the southwest corner of the Azad Maidan at Panjim is the Martyrs Memorial, a memorial built in honour of the martyrs who fought against the Portuguese rule.

Right: Closeup of the inscription at the base of the Martyrs Memorial, Azad Maidan, Panjim.

Facing page: This elegant building in Panjim was originally a summer palace built by Adil Shah in 1485.

and well-laid out streets. However, as destiny would have it, Yusuf Adil Shah was unable to hold on to this coveted possession for very long.

Arrival of the Portuguese

In 1498, Portuguese explorer Vasco da Gama first set foot in India, landing near Calicut on the Malabar Coast. His epic journey served to open up the spice trade between India and Portugal, and paved the way for further expeditions. Intent on strengthening their initial foothold so as to control sea route and trade links between Europe and Asia, the Portuguese ambition of establishing themselves firmly in India was soon to receive an unexpected boost. At the time, the Goan populace had begun to chafe under the rule of Yusuf Adil Shah. It seemed providential when Portuguese commander Afonso de Albuquerque was approached by a local person named Timmaya (known also as Timojja) asking for help to free Goa from the Adil Shah regime. Albuquerque gathered his forces together, and in early 1510 attacked Goa and managed to conquer it without much resistance.

But the Sultan of Bijapur was not about to take this defeat lightly. About two months later, in May 1510, he organized a massive attack and with the help of local Muslims managed to re-capture Goa. Afonso de Albuquerque and his men were forced to retreat and anchor down off the Mandovi, where they spent an uncomfortable few months at the mercy of the fierce south-west monsoon rains. Providentially though, additional ships and men arrived from Portugal just around that time. With these reinforcements, Albuquerque once again attacked Goa, conquering it on 25th November 1510. This time round, Albuquerque showed no mercy to the Muslims, hundreds of whom were slaughtered by his men. He had his soldiers marry local women, mostly widows of the slain Muslim soldiers, allotting land and gifts to those who did so. In honour of St. Catherine on whose Feast Day he had successfully conquered Goa, he built a chapel which still stands today besides the Archaeological Museum, close to the imposing Sé Cathedral at Old Goa. Albuquerque also set about reorganizing the administration and introduced several important legislations. He banned the horrific practice of sati (self-immolation by widows) and set up a Municipal Council called Senado de Goa (Senate of Goa). The Royal Hospital that was set up initially for the care of Albuquerque's own soldiers was later considered one of the best hospitals in the world.

In 1511, when Albuquerque left to capture Malacca, the Adilshahi ruler once again invaded Goa. On his return, however, Albuquerque successfully managed to expel the invaders. But Albuquerque's successes had garnered him many enemies and in 1515, in an unexpected development, a new Viceroy was appointed to supersede him, news that he received on board a ship on his way to Goa. Albuquerque, who was already ailing, died a few days later on 15th December 1515. As the ship sailed in to port, his last gaze was fixed on the land he loved so well. There is no doubt that Albuquerque had a special place in his heart for Goa and he was buried in the Chapel of Nossa Senhora de Serra which he had earlier built. Fifty years later, in 1565, his remains were taken back to Portugal. The city of Goa continued to prosper and flourish, attaining great heights in the areas of trade, art and architecture. Travellers visiting the city recounted amazing tales of its ostentation reflected in lavish lifestyles, rich opulence and grand buildings which led it to being called the 'Rome of the East.'

Spread of Christianity

Following the Portuguese conquest, various religious orders came to Goa. The Franciscans were amongst the first to arrive, followed by the Jesuits, the Dominicans, the Augustinians and others. They built huge religious edifices and using methods of persuasion and subtle pressure sought to convert the native population to the new religion. Soon harsher means were to follow. Orders were issued to destroy all Hindu temples in Portuguese controlled Goa, causing many to flee with their sacred deities and seek refuge in neighbouring areas. In 1560, the dreaded Inquisition was set up, its main aim being to punish those neo-converts who had embraced Christianity and yet still secretly practiced their old customs and traditions. Severe punishments were meted out to those who refused to accept the new doctrines. Even Konkani, the mother tongue of Goans was suppressed, and in fact banned in 1684. In the meantime, in spite of the opulence, or perhaps because of it, corruption, depravity and moral decadence took root in the capital city. Finally, a combination of economic factors and unsanitary conditions led to its inevitable decline. Not only were the city's drainage systems inadequate, but epidemics of cholera and plague broke out, killing hundreds. In 1707, the capital was shifted to Panjim and several edifices were pulled down to provide building material for the new capital.

The territory that was known as Goa in those days was not

the same as the present-day Goa. Warring with neighbouring rulers continued for decades, which resulted in frequently changing territorial boundaries. The areas of Tiswadi, Bardez, Salcete and Mormugao which were first acquired by the Portuguese were called the Old Conquests or *Velhas Conquistas*; much later were the territories of Pernem, Bicholim, Ponda, Sattari, Sanguem, Quepem and Canacona acquired, which came to be known as the New Conquests or *Novas Conquistas*. Goa continued to suffer frequent attacks by the Dutch and the Marathas while the British also tried to impose their designs on the land. By the mid-1800s, however, Portuguese attitudes had become somewhat more liberal. After constitutional monarchy was established in 1822, Portugal even had two Goan members of Parliament and later on, Goans were also given citizenship rights. Goa is today the only state in the country to have a Uniform Civil Code applicable to all persons irrespective of religion, another legacy of the Portuguese administration.

The Freedom Movement

The Portuguese rule was punctuated by several revolts over the years by both Christians and Hindus seeking to free themselves from the foreign yoke. However, these were quickly nipped in the bud often with severe reprisals.

Soon after India attained independence in 1947, a mission was sent to Lisbon to negotiate withdrawal from Goa. But the Portuguese refused to cede Goa, maintaining that it was a part of its domain. The Government of India retaliated by imposing an economic blockade on Goa, in 1955. Finally, in December 1961 prime minister Jawahar Lal Nehru ordered a military invasion of Goa. With little resistance from Portuguese troops, Goa along with the territories of Daman and Diu was liberated on 19th December 1961.

The Goa of Today

Goa was accorded the status of a full-fledged state on 30th May 1987. Of late, however, frequent changes in government have resulted in a certain amount of political instability. Even so, Goa still maintains its distinctive identity and today Goans can be found throughout the world in the top echelons of art, music, literature, medicine and other fields.

Above: The Portuguese & Franciscans built huge religious edifices and used methods of persuasion to convert the native population to Christianity.

Facing page: A veritable cliff-top citadel, Fort Aguada was constructed by the Portuguese in 1612 in defense against Dutch and Maratha invaders.

Previous page: Elaborate azulejo tile panel at the Menezes Braganza Institute at Panjim, depicting Venus with frollicking sea-nymphs whom the Portuguese seamen were envisioned to have encountered on their voyages.

In And Around Goa

Goa has often been described as a melting pot of different cultures, a description that is surely as apt today as it ever was. Not only has the region been shaped by past influences, but even today diverse factors continue to exert their influence on Goan society. Yet, the Goan lifestyle has still retained an endearing distinctiveness and character that is unmistakable. As you travel around the cities and the villages you can feel it in the long-standing cultural traditions, in the creative expressions of art, architecture, music and dance, and in the relaxed way of life and the friendly attitudes that are so much a part of Goa.

Urban Hubs

The capital of Goa is Panjim or Panaji as it is officially designated. This brings us to the rather peculiar fact, often a source of confusion to visitors, that the same place in Goa is known by different names. Mostly, it is just linguistic variation that accounts for the seemingly differing names. For example, though officially named Panaji, Goa's capital is most commonly referred to as Ponjje in colloquial Konkani or as Panjim by the English speaker. It may be even more confusing to learn that during Portuguese times it was called Pangim.

By whatever name it is known though, Panjim still remains a delightful city with its own distinctive character. From the Altinho hilltop you get a bird's eye view of the city. Brightly painted houses and little lanes in the old quarters of Sao Tome and Fontainhas evoke an atmosphere of old-world charm. In the commercial heart of the city lie some of its landmarks including the Summer Palace built by Adil Shah, the statue of Abbé Faria, the Church of the Immaculate Conception with its double staircase, the Central Library and the Police Head Quarters located close to the Azad Maidan, the Mahalaxmi temple and the Boca de Vaca spring close by. Further down at Campal is the Kala Academy, an academy of music, art and culture. As you travel past the Miramar beach and the Goa Science Centre and on to

Above: This terracotta sculpture on a traffic isle at Panjim, by Mapusa-based Verodina de Souza e Ferrao, is not only a beautiful artistic depiction, but also a tribute to the Goan fisherwoman.

Top: Brightly painted houses and little lanes in the old quarters of Sao Tome and Fontainhas evoke an atmosphere of old-world charm.

One of the best known landmarks in Goa is an intriguing statue at Panjim of a person in flowing robes, arms outstretched and bent over the figure of a prostrate woman. The statue, crafted by the talented Goan sculptor Ramachandra Pandurang Kamat, is that of Abbé Faria (also known as Abade Faria), a native Goan who later came to be recognised worldwide as the 'father of modern hypnotism.' Abbé Faria also played a part in the earliest attempts to overthrow the Portuguese rule in Goa and his story is fascinating indeed. Born in Candolim in 1756 to Caetano Vitorino de Faria and Maria Rosa de Souza, the boy was named José Custódio de Faria. When still a child, his parents separated by mutual consent – interestingly, after being granted the necessary ecclesiastical permission, both his father and mother opted for religious careers. His father, who had earlier aspired to become a priest, joined the priesthood and was subsequently ordained, while his mother entered the Santa Monica convent where she later became the prioress. Both father and son went to Portugal in 1771. José too studied for the priesthood and on being ordained a priest at Rome came to be known as Abbé Faria. There is an interesting tale about an incident that took place around that time. Invited to deliver a lecture at the Royal Chapel in Lisbon, José reportedly became tongue-tied with nervousness as he stood before the august assembly. Whereupon his father, who was also in the audience, urged him on with the words in Konkani, "*He sogle kator re bhaji!*" meaning "All these are (just) vegetables! Cut the vegetables!" Hearing this, José confidently delivered a brilliant lecture that had his audience absolutely enthralled. After some unsuccessful attempts to overthrow the Portuguese in Goa, attempts in which he played a significant role, José fled to France. There he studied magnetism, and put forth many original theories about hypnotism that disproved those in vogue at the time. Several authors were inspired enough to refer to him in their works, including French novelist Alexandre Dumas, who immortalized him as a character in his novel 'The Count of Monte Carlo'. Abbé Faria died in 1819, and the statue at Panjim was erected in his honour in 1945.

Dona Paula, you pass the National Institute of Oceanography and the Raj Bhavan, the palatial residence of Goa's governor.

Mapusa, situated about 12 kilometres north of Panjim, is a bustling town, best known for its Friday market where all kinds of wares are sold. Practically all the villages and beaches of North Goa are accessible via Mapusa. One of the city's best known landmarks is the Bodgeshwar temple; others are the Hanuman Theatre just opposite the temple, the High Court and of course, the Municipal market.

Ponda is best known for the many temples in its surrounding villages. There are also several spice farms close by, making it a draw for tourists wanting to combine a visit to the temples and a spice farm. With many shops, small factories and industrial units around, it is also an industrial hub and business district.

Margao, situated in the Salcete Taluka about 32 kilometres from Panjim, is a veritable hub of commercial activity. Centered around a large public park are shops and offices, the main Post Office, the Collector's Office and the Municipality building. A short distance away are the main bazaar and the fish market (recently re-located near the main bus stand) - both usually bustle with activity from mid-morning to late evening. Margao's biggest church, the Church of the Holy Spirit, overlooks the old central square called the Largo de Igreja. Close by are several well-preserved old-style houses, the biggest of which is the Silva Mansion at Borda. Goa's main railway terminus is also located at Margao.

Above: Originally a fortress guarding the mouth of the Mandovi, this palatial building at Dona Paula is the residence of the Governor of Goa.

Top: Seat of the Goa Government, the Secretariat earlier functioned from the Adil Shah Palace at Panjim and was more recently shifted to the present premises at Porvorim.

Facing page: Sun, sea and graceful palm trees... Goa, as idyllic as it gets...

Vasco da Gama, located about 30 kilometres from Panjim, is more of an industrial and commercial city. It has its own railway station while the airport is just a few kilometres away. The Goa Shipyard is located in the city environs while the Mormugao Port Trust carries on ore-handling and other operations at the nearby Mormugao Harbour. A significant number of migrants from other states now live here, attracted mainly to the employment opportunities in the various industries.

Rural Scape

The essence of Goa lies in its picturesque villages, where the lifestyle is peaceful and unhurried. Here is where Goa's distinctive culture and customs have been preserved over centuries. Dotted with red-roofed houses, the countryside is a charming picture of emerald paddy fields fringed with coconut palms. The beginning of the monsoon season sees farmers skillfully guiding their oxen as they plough the fields before sowing time. Once the harvest is over, the fields are often planted with local vegetables that later find their way to urban markets.

Geography

Goa has an area of 3,702 square kilometres. The state of Maharashtra lies to its north and Karnataka to its south. To the east is the richly forested Sahayadri mountain range, and to the west lies the Arabian Sea. Goa's main rivers are the Mandovi and Zuari; others include the Tiracol, Chapora, Sal, Talpona and Galgibaga rivers.

Climate

Goa has a balmy, tropical climate. From October to March the days are sunny and warm (22°C-32°C) though in December and January, one might feel a slight nip in the air, in the evenings. From March to May the temperature and the

humidity rise (25°C-33°C) till the monsoon breaks in June, bringing a welcome relief from the heat. The rains continue from June right through to September when the air is crisp and clean and the smell of the rain-drenched earth assails the senses as the entire countryside is transformed into a verdant green landscape.

Administration

For administrative purposes, Goa is divided into two districts – North Goa and South Goa. These are further divided into eleven *talukas* – Bardez, Salcete, Ponda, Bicholim, Canacona, Pernem, Quepem, Sanguem, Tiswadi, Sattari and Mormugao. The Secretariat, seat of the Goa Government, was earlier housed at the Adil Shah Palace at Panjim, but now functions from more spacious premises at the Porvorim Assembly Complex.

Language

Konkani, the mellifluous language spoken by practically all Goans, is the State's official language, with use of Marathi allowed for all official purposes. English is, however, widely spoken and understood everywhere. Portuguese is still spoken by a few, while the national language Hindi is also understood by most.

Above: *In the Lamp dance, participants move with intricate steps and complex yet graceful movements, while skillfully balancing lighted brass lamps on their heads.*

This page, top: *The* mando *is usually a love song as well as an elevated dance form where the ladies holding fans in their right hands, sway sensuously to the music while casting coquettish glances at their partners.*

Facing page, top: *Sea, sand and sports... a long stretch of uncrowded beach seems to be a great place to catch up on a game of cricket.*

Facing page, bottom: *A fisherman skillfully casting his net into the sea.*

Sport

Though cricket is fast becoming as popular as it already is in other parts of the country, football still remains the favourite sport in Goa. A familiar sight all over Goa, especially during the summer season, is that of village lads having a friendly game in the open fields cheered on by enthusiastic spectators. Several of these youth later go on to become players for top football clubs. Goa, too, has several excellent football clubs like Salgaocar Sports Club, Dempo Sports Club, Churchill Brothers, Vasco Sports Club, Fransa Pax, etc. Many of Goa's footballers and football clubs have distinguished themselves in the National Football League and other prestigious tournaments.

Cultural Traditions

Music and dance are an integral part of Goa's rich cultural heritage. Goan folk music has a lively, catchy rhythm while the folk dances exhibit an energetic vitality and joie de vivre. Musical accompaniment is provided using instruments like the *ghumat*, *dhol*, harmonium, violin and guitar.

Popular folk dances include the *Fugdi* and the *Dhalo* performed by women. In the *Fugdi*, women dance in a circular fashion with rhythmic steps that begin slowly and move on to a faster pace. In the *Dhalo*, two parallel rows of women dance rhythmically towards each other.

The Lamp dance usually has onlookers awed as the participants move with intricate steps and complex yet graceful movements, while skillfully balancing lighted brass lamps on their heads. The *Ghode Modni* is essentially a war dance, where a figure of a wooden horse is attached to the waist of the performers who brandish swords while moving rhythmically to recreate the prancing of horses.

The *Corredinho* is an elegant Portuguese folk dance where couples in colourful Western costumes move in a rhythmic, eye-catching manner, while the *Kunbi* dance is a popular harvest dance. The *Musoll* or pestle dance is a legacy of the Kadamba past and is performed in Chandor on the second day of Carnival by Christian Kshatriya dancers dressed in native Hindu costumes.

The *Goff* dance associated with the heralding of spring, involves the braiding of different coloured cords into a colourful plait through skillful dance steps. Each dancer holds one end of a coloured cord hanging from a central point, and moves in intricate steps with the other dancers, forming a

multi-coloured braid. The dancers then skillfully reverse the pattern so that the braid gets unravelled and all the cords are separate once again.

The *Dekhni* combines western rhythm with ethnic melody. A very popular rendition is performed to the captivating melody of the song '*Aum saiba poltodi vetam.*' The song is apparently sung by a temple dancing girl requesting a boatman to take her across the river. The dance is enlivened as the girl and her companions coax, cajole and entreat the boatman to ferry them across the river, and the haunting strains of the song remain with you long after the performance is over.

The *mando* is essentially an evocative song, most often a love song, with soul-stirring lyrics. The *mando* is also an elevated dance form where a file of men stands at some distance from that of the women. The ladies, holding fans in their right hands, sway sensuously to the music. The men move handkerchiefs, stylishly held with the fingers of both hands, up and down according to the rhythm of the music. As they advance and retreat to the quickening rhythm, the movement is that of courtship; the mock-passionate glances of the men provoke a shy, coquettish response in the women. The *mando* is followed by the livelier beat and quickening rhythm

of the *dulpod*. The *mando* was earlier very popular at occasions like weddings and other social events.

Tiatr is a form of popular entertainment unique to Goa, a form of drama based mostly on social, political and religious themes. The plays are interspersed with songs and the mix of drama and song makes it quite popular amongst the masses. *Zagor*, on the other hand, is an age-old folk festival performed at night by Hindus and Christians in the sacred open space, or *maand* in the village, and is considered to be a precursor of modern-day theatre. The actors are exclusively men and the themes chosen provide earthy entertainment to the hundreds who come to watch. The *Perni Zagor*, performed by the Perni community is a form of dance-drama in which painted wooden masks are used.

The Tourist Trail

Goa has all kinds of experiences to offer its visitors. Set foot in Goa and you can immediately sense a change in the pace of life, an unhurried cadence that allows you to relax and unwind. In Goa, the *socegado* way of doing things at one's own pace is a welcome contrast to the stressful hurry and rush elsewhere. The sunny weather from mid-October to May is perfect for spending time at the beach, while the monsoon months of June to September allow you to experience a different side of Goa, when the summer canopy of leaves interspersed with gold, red and brown turns a refreshing shade of green and everything around seems rejuvenated with new life. Whether you want to go bird watching or trekking, visit the markets or just lounge around on the beach: there is always something in Goa to suit your style, your interests and your budget.

Above: Basking in the sun, soaking in the warmth of Goa.

Facing page, top: Water sports are popular in Goa; a ride in a speed boat is exhilarating.

Facing page, bottom: Enjoying the thrill of para-sailing.

Beguiling Beaches

With so many miles of beautiful coastline, it is probably no surprise that the first thing that most visitors want to do when they reach Goa is to head for the beach. From Pernem in the north to Canacona in the south lies an entire stretch of palm-fringed golden beaches and enchanting little coves and bays that beckon ever so invitingly. If it's a peaceful getaway you are looking for, take your pick from quieter and more tranquil beaches like those of Keri, Mandrem, Ashwem and Morjim in the northern part of Goa or Velsao, Arossim, Utorda, Majorda, Betalbatim, Benaulim and Agonda in the south. Lie on the warm sands, listening to the sound of the waves as they break and then roll up to the shore with a frothy swish. Feel a sense of serenity wash over your soul as you watch the gulls skimming over the water and the fishing boats silhouetted against the horizon. The scenic beaches of Arambol in Pernem and Palolem in Canacona which were earlier peaceful, secluded spots have now begun to attract more and more people. The Colva beach close to Margao is pretty and one of the most popular beaches of South Goa, often somewhat crowded during the high season.

If it's a really lively scene that you are looking for, then head for the coastal hotspots like Calangute, Anjuna, Vagator, Baga and Sinquerim in the northern belt. During the high season these beaches, though crowded, fairly throb with life. A variety of cuisine is on offer at the beach shacks and restaurants close by, and the music belting out ranges from rave to retro with live entertainment often thrown in. Once known as the 'Queen of beaches,' Calangute beach is now rather crowded, though you can still enjoy the sea and sand. And if people-watching is your scene then this is the perfect place to treat yourself to a cool drink at one of the nearby shacks while you sit back, relax and simply watch the world go by.

Anjuna beach was a favourite haunt of the flower generation of the sixties and though it is still popular, Anjuna is better known for its Wednesday Flea Market. Vagator has a more attractive, crescent-shaped beach flanked by rocky cliffs that overlook the shore. On the far left of the Vagator beach close to the shoreline, is an impressive sculpture of the face of Lord Shiva carved on a large seaside rock. Said to be the work of a Westerner who'd spent some months there in a meditative mood, the sculpture makes for an unusual picture as the

River Cruises

Cruising along the river Mandovi, on board the Santa Monica owned by the Goa Tourism Development Corporation, is a delightful way to spend an evening in Goa. Other private operators also organize cruises. The hour-long trips leave from the Patto jetty, near the foot of the Mandovi bridge at Panjim, cruise down the river till just off Miramar and then return. There is lively on-board cultural entertainment with music and folk dances and you might even get a chance to shake a leg before the trip winds up.

Dolphin and Crocodile Quest

If you've ever yearned to watch dolphins frolicking in their natural habitat, a dolphin-spotting cruise is the perfect trip for you. Several operators organize trips where you are guaranteed a sight of these playful creatures. To watch them gambol around your boat and leap in graceful curves over the sparkling blue waters is an enchanting experience. Crocodile spotting trips are also available where you can cruise slowly down the backwaters and catch a glimpse of the crocodiles sunning themselves on the muddy banks of the river.

incoming waves swirl gently around the serene face of Shiva. Apart from its beach, Baga has a choice of restaurants and the nightlife too is the liveliest around, with plenty of places to party at. These are only a few of Goa's beaches; there are scores of others where you can experience the sand and surf at its loveliest best.

Adventure Sports

Over the past few years adventure sports have really caught on, and those seeking an adrenaline-rush have plenty to be thrilled about. With all adventure sports, one has to be careful and ensure that all necessary safety precautions are observed. But from water sports to trekking to go-carting, there's lots of action to be had in Goa. The beautiful coastline is ideal for activities like water skiing, jet-skiing, para-sailing, speedboat rides, catamaran and hobie cat sailing, windsurfing, snorkeling and scuba diving. Also popular are banana, bump and ringo rides where you sit in an air-filled rubber craft tied to a speedboat and go on an exhilarating ride over the waves. The most popular places for water sports are Dona Paula, the stretch from Calangute to Sinquerim and the beaches at Bogmalo, Arrosim, Majorda and Mobor. Go-carting tracks at Arpora in North Goa and Nuvem in South Goa let you unleash the fiend in you as you step on the accelerator and zoom along the tracks. For the avid trekker, the Goa Hiking Association, the Youth Hostels Association of India and other nature clubs often organize hikes and treks in the lush interiors.

Wellness Therapies

The newest attractions on offer to Goa's visitors are a range of wellness therapies. From aromatherapy and ayurveda to meditation and yoga on the beach, all kinds of alternative treatments seem to be available. It is best though, to go with reliable, qualified and trained practitioners such as those attached to hotels and resorts. Most of the starred hotels offer ayurvedic massages and other treatments in addition to sauna and spa experiences also. Several resorts also conduct courses in yoga, meditation, reiki, *pranic* healing and other alternative therapies.

Spice Farms

Back in the olden days, traders and merchants from far-off lands were drawn to India by the lure of exotic spices which not only enhanced the taste of food, but were also used in the making of perfumes and for their medicinal value. The discovery that spices retained their flavour after drying and hence could be transported and stored for long periods, led to an increased demand and fierce battles were fought as several nations sought to gain monopoly of this lucrative trade. Spices were also widely cultivated in Goa and this region too became a destination for voyagers from across the seas. Though they are now much more easily available globally than they were

then, today the spice farms in Goa attract large numbers of tourists eager to see how various spices are grown. A visit to a spice farm is a delightful experience and a definite must for any visitor. Interestingly, the entrance charge at most farms includes a guided tour as well as delectable snacks and a delicious lunch. You can also watch Goan folk dances, though this is arranged only on prior request.

Whilst there are spice farms scattered all over Goa, there is a cluster around the Ponda area, which is also on the tourist circuit due to its beautiful temples. The spice plantations in this area include the Savoi Plantation, the Sahakari Spice Farm and the Pascoal Spice Village. Most farms have trained guides to take you on a tour of the plantation, where you get to see various herbs and spices under cultivation like pepper, turmeric, lemongrass, ginger, basil, curry leaves, nutmeg, cloves, cardamom, cinnamon, vanilla, etc. The guides also explain their uses and medicinal properties.

About 12 kilometres away from Ponda is the Savoi Plantation, located in the sleepy village of Savoi Verem. As you enter, you are welcomed with a garland of flowers and treated to delectable snacks and a refreshing drink of fresh tender coconut water. On your tour around the farm, apart from being shown the spices that are grown there, you also get to see a cashew *feni* distillation unit and a vermi-composting unit as well. It is fascinating to

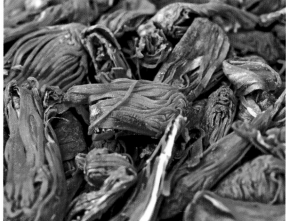

Anticlockwise from the top: *Several spices are locally grown in Goa including star anise, vanilla and mace. Incidentally, vanilla is the second most expensive spice in the world after saffron.*

Facing page: *Cruising along the River Mandovi is a delightful way to spend an evening in Goa.*

watch arecanuts being plucked from the trees by a plucker who nimbly springs across from one tree-top to another. Lunch is a superb, mouth-watering spread of Goan Saraswat cuisine served in traditional mud pots and eaten on banana leaves placed on bamboo platters followed by dessert. One can also purchase spice powders and other items grown or prepared here.

The Sahakari Spice Farm is located at Curti, Ponda on the Ponda-Belgaum highway, and has a total area of 130 acres. Here too one receives a traditional welcome, snacks, tender coconut water and lemon grass tea. The farm has a cashew *feni* distillation unit, a cashew nut processing unit and a small dairy with several cross-breed cows. The cowshed is interconnected to a bio-gas plant and a compost pit, so that optimal use is made of the waste dung. There are also a couple of elephants on the farm which is an added attraction for visitors as you can not only go on an elephant ride, but also help wash them too. Lunch is a feast of Goan dishes served in mud pots and eaten on banana leaves, followed by fresh fruits for dessert. The Sahakari Farm also has a sale counter where you can make your purchases of different spices, oil extracts, dried vanilla pods, etc.

The Pascoal Spice Village is located at Khandepar, about 7 kilometres away from Ponda, on the Ponda-Usgao Road. If you are a plant lover, you will surely be fascinated by the wide variety of plants, both flowering and non-flowering, that are grown there apart from the spices. There are several attractive bonsai and a large nursery with plants on sale. A small rivulet runs through the place, adding to its idyllic charm. You can sit awhile on the banks feeding the fish or if you so wish, you could spend a little longer time paddling on the water as boating facilities are also available. The charming restaurant on the farm serves Goan and other dishes.

Other spice farms in the area include Abyss and Tropical Spice Plantation.

Forts

If you are interested in a bit of history, you would probably enjoy clambering over the ruins of some of Goa's old forts. There are a great many located all over Goa, built to protect against the various invaders of the times. Some of these are the forts at Aguada, Chapora, Reis Magos and Terekhol in North Goa, Mormugao in the Mormugao Taluka and Cabo de Rama in Canacona. The North Goa forts of Aguada, Chapora and Terekhol are the ones most frequented by tourists.

Strategically built to defend the Aguada Bay and the mouth of the Mandovi river, Fort Aguada was constructed by the Portuguese in 1612 to defend themselves against Dutch and Maratha invaders. One of the strongest bastions, Fort Aguada never fell despite several fierce battles. The fort derives its name on account of the freshwater springs located within (the name Aguada comes from *agua*, which in Portuguese means water). It was from these springs that ships in those days replenished their freshwater supplies. There is a lighthouse and a church within its precincts, and as you walk across the wide moat and up the ramparts, you can feel the tug of ancient history as you delight in breathtaking views of the bay and of the sea.

Originally built by the Adil Shah Sultans, the Chapora Fort is thought to have derived its name from the word 'Shahpura', meaning 'City of the Shah,' as the village of Chapora was once believed to have been known. The Portuguese rebuilt this fort in 1717 on the remains of the original battlements. The fort was taken over for a short time by marauding Maratha warriors led by Sambhaji, son of the Maratha chief Shivaji, but was subsequently returned to the Portuguese in exchange for Bassein, near Bombay. Now in ruins, the fort offers impressive views of the coastline below.

The Terekhol Fort near the Terekhol river at the northern tip of Goa offers magnificent views coupled with age-old history. Originally built by the Bhonsles, a Maratha clan, the fort was captured in 1746 by the Portuguese Viceroy, Dom Pedro Miguel de Almeida, and later rebuilt. High embattlements face the sea and a small chapel is set in the courtyard. The fort has now been converted into a heritage hotel. Each room has spectacular sea views and in the stillness one can hear the muted sound of waves crashing onto the rocks below.

Museums

There are several museums in Goa that showcase different aspects of Goa's past. These include the Goa State Museum at Patto-Panjim, the Archaeological Museum and Portrait Gallery, the Sound and Light Gallery and the Museum of Christian Art at Old Goa, and the Pilar Seminary Museum at Pilar. Incidentally, in the same complex at Pilar is the marble mausoleum housing the remains of Ven. Fr. Agnelo, a devout Goan priest whose canonization process towards sainthood is presently underway. There is also a tiny museum at the Blessed Joseph Vaz Sanctuary, at Sancoale. Declared as the patron of Goa a few years back, the canonization process of Blessed Joseph Vaz is also underway.

The museum 'Houses of Goa' at Torda, Salvador de Mundo, Bardez documents Indo-Portuguese domestic architecture. Close by, at the Xavier Centre of Historical Research, Porvorim is a small gallery on Christian art.

Goa has several artists and sculptors of excellent calibre. Some of their works are on display at private galleries like Gallery Gitanjali at Fontainhas-Panjim, Art Chamber

Above: A veritable cliff-top citadel, Fort Aguada was constructed by the Portuguese in 1612 in defense against Dutch and Maratha invaders.

Facing page, top: Migrant vendors from nearby states are often seen selling wares on the beaches.

Facing page, bottom: The liveliness of Goa is infectious and goes beyond the beaches. Fun and frolick is a way of life.

(Galeria de Belas Artes) at Calangute, Kerkar Art Complex also at Calangute and at Galeria Cidade, at Hotel Cidade de Goa, Dona Paula.

The Naval Aviation Museum, located about 2 kilometres from the Dabolim Airport on the Bogmalo Road, has a fascinating indoor and outdoor display of memorabilia from India's naval aviation history. The outdoor display features vintage planes like the Alize, Hughes, Vampire T55, Sea Hawk, Fire Fly, Sea Land, Dove, Chetak, Hindustan Trainer HT2 and Sea Harrier aircraft.

A large collection of vintage cars (including Mercedes Benz, Peugeot, Chevrolet, Morris, Volkswagen) is on display on all week days at Ashvek Vintage World, near the chapel of Our Lady of Vailankanni, at Nuvem, Salcete.

Shopping

Delightful souvenirs and gift items can be found in most of the bigger towns as well as in the stores and stalls that dot the coastal villages. The Goa government handicraft emporiums stock all kinds of items made of shell, bamboo and jute, coconut shell items, brass and lacquer work, wood and fibre-stone carvings and of course, the terracotta items made by

that started somewhere in the '70s when cash-strapped hippies from the West began selling their belongings at an impromptu market to make some money to meet their needs. In those days, goods for sale included music systems, cameras, radios, guitars, jeans, scarves, shoes and other sundry personal items and people thronged there hoping to chance upon a good bargain. Today the market has diversified and one now sees foreigners as well as Rajasthani, Gujarati, Kashmiri, Lamani and a few local vendors selling all kinds of goods, from freshly ground spices, bandanas and bedcovers to jewellery, handicrafts and electronic items. The market is a whole day affair, beginning mid-morning and going on till evening, and is a draw for tourists looking to enjoy the vibrant atmosphere of the Flea Market and to pick up some bargains. Even more happening is Ingo's Saturday Nite Market at Arpora, which begins early Saturday evening and goes on till midnight. The atmosphere is pulsating and vibrant as you are confronted with an incredible melee of goods. Foreigners as well as vendors from all over India seem to sell anything and everything from the exotic to the mundane. Browse through stalls that have various kinds of bric-a-brac that include Pashmina shawls, ethnic outfits with Rajasthani mirror work, handmade shoes, music compact discs, stone and wooden artifacts, a variety of trinkets, bags, funky tee shirts, wall hangings, leather masks, musical instruments, pewter mugs and exquisite items in silver. It's a heady eclectic mix where tattoo artists and fortune tellers add their own quixotic touch to the atmosphere. There is also an outdoor food court where you can enjoy live entertainment centre stage while you sample gastronomic delights that range from Japanese sushi and Italian pasta to German pastries and Goan *cafreal*. Both the Anjuna Flea Market and Ingo's Saturday Nite Market are open only during the high season from mid-October to around mid-March. Both the Anjuna Flea Market and Ingo's Saturday Nite Market are open only during the high season from mid-October to around mid-March. Other night markets are Mackies, at Arpora also on Saturday nights, and the Colva Night Market at Colva on Monday nights.

Apart from the usual markets in every village and town, some places have weekly bazaars either on Sundays or on other particular days of the week. The best known of these is the Friday Market, at Mapusa. Here the lively hustle and bustle of the marketplace is as much an attraction as the wares on sale. As the vendors converge early on Friday mornings and

the famed potters of Bicholim. Portuguese *azulejos* art in the form of glazed decorative tiles, with characteristic blue-and-white motifs portraying Goan themes, are also available. *Feni*, Goa's famed liquor, is a popular buy, often packaged in miniature bottles of attractive shapes and sizes. Roasted cashew nuts are also a particular favourite with several different varieties available. Browse around the stores and you're sure to find some unusual item or other to pick up.

Market Day

The Wednesday Flea Market at Anjuna is a colourful affair

Above: Off the beaten track – ancient rock art in Goa seen at Pansaimol in the Sanguem Taluka, located on the banks of the river Khushavati.

Top:Handicraft items and trinkets on display at the Anjuna Flea Market.

Facing page: On the far left of the Vagator beach is an impressive sculpture of the face of Lord Shiva carved on a large seaside rock, said to be the work of a Westerner in a meditative mood.

Previous page: Shoppers enjoy the vibrant thrill of the Wednesday Flea market at Anjuna.

ropes, the brown triangular mounds of Goa's unique palm jaggery, an assortment of the local bread, pickles, red chillies and of course 'chouriço' or 'chouris,' Goa's tantalizingly spicy sausage. One can also pick up inexpensive tee-shirts, shorts and all kinds of trinkets over here.

Off the Beaten Track

The finding of several specimens of rare, age-old rock art in Goa has been a significant discovery indeed. An important part of Goa's heritage, these specimens, dating back hundreds of years, are an illustration of man's creativity and desire to express himself even in ancient times. One of the best examples of rock art in Goa is seen at Pansaimol in the Sanguem Taluka, located on the banks of the river Khushavati. Though weatherworn over the centuries, one can still make out several distinct motifs carved on the rocks. These include a humped bull, a peacock, a concentric maze, a dancing girl, other human figures and various animals and birds. Prajal Sakhardande, history lecturer and member of the Goa Heritage Action Group says, "These are examples of rich, prehistoric rock art known as petroglyphs. Prehistoric rock art in Goa is also seen at Mauxi in the Sattari Taluka besides Kazur and Pirla in the Quepem Taluka. In the book 'Ancient Civilizations: World Heritage Sites' by Marco Cattaneo and Jasmina Trifoni, the authors talk of several such ancient rock art sites found in other parts of the world. These include the Cueva de Las Manos in the Rio Pinturas Valley of Argentina, the Serra da Capivara

begin to unload their wares, the market starts to hum with activity. Walk through the inner lanes to experience the true flavour of a local market. Fresh fish as well as locally grown fresh vegetables and a whole variety of fruits are on sale including the famed jumbo bananas from Moira. All kinds of commodities seem to be available here and you can find a selection of items that includes plants, earthenware, coir mats,

(located behind the main Panjim bus stand at Patto, close to the LIC building).

Several small rock-cut caves have also been discovered at various sites in Goa, including Khandepar, Arvalem, Narve and Rivona. Scrutiny by experts suggests that they may have been Buddhist or *Brahmanical* caves and were either religious shrines or possibly the abode of hermits. In his book 'Inside Goa', Manohar Malgonkar describes the Arvalem caves saying, "Perhaps the best preserved are the caves at Arvalem, excavated in the

in Brazil, the painted grottoes in the Vallee de la Vezere in France and the megalithic monuments of the Boyne Valley in Ireland." Closer home we have the Bimbetka rock paintings, near Bhopal. Researchers estimate that the site at Pansaimol is about 8000 to 9000 years old, belonging to the Mesolithic Period and the carvings were probably done with specially made, sharp stone tools. Casual visitors may find it a bit tedious travelling so far to the remote interiors, and might instead prefer to view a realistic model of the site at the Goa State Museum

hillside and overlooking a ravine through which flows one of the smaller streams of Goa. There are three main caves and a few smaller ones tucked on all sides which suggests that they may have been used for some kind of a small religious colony. The three main caves are in a line, and one of them has three chambers, like rooms in a house, with the roof supported by pillars hewn out of laterite. On a small platform in the innermost room rests a stone *linga*." Clearly, many interesting aspects of Goa's history are yet to be unearthed and studied.

There are several options for travelling around in Goa. The most comfortable, though also the most expensive, is to hire a car to take you around. For shorter distances, you could also travel by the black-and-yellow auto rickshaws; unfortunately, they rarely charge by the meter as they ought to, and one should therefore confirm the price beforehand.

Buses are generally crowded, except in the case of the relatively comfortable shuttle service between the main towns. A ride on the flat-bottomed ferries that ply across some of the rivers is also fascinating. You could also hire a self-drive vehicle, though with the prevailing chaotic traffic conditions, this may not be really advisable. One of the most interesting ways to getting around, especially for short trips, is to travel by Goa's quaint motorcycle taxis. These are a cheap and fun way to travel. Like the usual taxi stands, there are stands for the motorcycles too, and as you approach the riders rev up the engines of their motorcycles in anticipation. Not o nly do they charge a pretty reasonable fare, but as you hop on behind the rider you are free to gaze around and enjoy the feel of the wind in your hair as you zoom to your destination.

Above : *Migrant vendors at the Saturday Night market help a buyer try out toe rings for size.*

Top: *Fishing trawlers anchored on the River Mandovi, just across from Panjim.*

Sacred Places

Religion is an important part of life in Goa, almost imperceptibly interwoven as it were, into the fabric of daily living. Travel around anywhere in the State, and you cannot help but notice the innumerable wayside shrines, crosses, temples and churches that dot the landscape. According to the 2001 statistics, Goa has a Hindu majority that accounts for 65.8% of the total population of about 1.34 million. Of the rest, Christians make up about 26.7%, Muslims another 6.8%, while other religious faiths comprise about 0.7%. Yet, the communal amity and open-mindedness that might seem remarkable anywhere else in the country, is just a way of life in Goa where it is not uncommon to find people of different communities worshipping at the same shrine. In fact, it has been remarked that in Goa the chime of the church bell blends easily with the tinkle of the temple bell in a kind of divine harmony.

Above: *The Corinthian interior of the Se Cathedral at Old Goa, where the main altar is dedicated to St. Catherine.*

Facing page: *The magnificient facade of the Church of Our Lady of Immaculate Conception at Panjim, with its unusual zig-zag double staircase.*

Churches

Having been built by various European monastic orders, much of the architecture of Goa's churches is obviously based on European styles. However, classic forms were adapted to suit the local climate and sensibilities, resulting in an impressive amalgam of structural styles. Local craftsmen were employed in building these churches and consequently some of the decorative features and motifs done by them bear a startling resemblance to the traditional Hindu designs that they were earlier habituated to crafting. Thus, many of these churches exhibit, especially in the interiors, a delightful blend of European and Indian craftsmanship, motifs and aesthetics.

Though Goa is endowed with several magnificent churches, it is the Basilica of Bom Jesus (1594 –1605) at Old Goa which is especially revered since it houses the sacred relics of St. Francis Xavier. Built by the Jesuits, this grand Baroque structure with a three-tiered laterite façade has three doors on its frontispiece which open onto a single spacious rectangular nave. The main altar, magnificently gilded in gold, is dedicated to the Infant Jesus above whose image stands another much larger one of St. Ignatius de Loyola, right hand upraised. To the left of the altar, on the northern side, is the Chapel of the Blessed Sacrament. In the south chapel to the right of the altar, on top of a marble mausoleum, is the jewel-studded silver reliquary containing the glass casket with the sacred relics of St. Francis Xavier. The reliquary was designed by an Italian Jesuit priest and crafted by Goan silversmiths. Glass panels allow a glimpse of the relics to the thousands of pilgrims who come to visit, while below are panels that depict scenes from the life of the saint. The marble mausoleum, gifted by the grand Duke of Tuscany in exchange for a pillow that had lain under the head of the saint, was executed by Florentine sculptor Giovanni Batista Foggini and then sent to Goa and assembled in 1698. Winged angels adorn the top portion which is supported by Corinthian columns resting on the marble base. As a matter of fact, there are many age-old churches, chapels, monuments and a couple of museums at Old Goa and if one has the time and the inclination many rewarding moments can be spent in exploring historic landmarks that speak of the timeless wonders of an age gone by. Walk under the Arch of the Viceroys, visit the Churches of St. Cajetan and Our Lady of the Rosary, and admire the scenic views from the recently restored Chapel of Our Lady of Monte. Take a look at the ruins of the once-magnificent St. Augustine's Tower that long ago stood sentinel over the city. But if time is a constraint, you could perhaps visit just the Sé Cathedral and the Church of St. Francis of Assisi, both within walking distance of the Basilica of Bom Jesus.

The Sé Cathedral built over a period from 1562-1619 is Asia's largest church and has a Tuscan exterior. Its Corinthian interior has a main grand high altar dedicated to St. Catherine, eight chapels along the aisles and six altars in the transept. One of the chapels houses a wooden cross said to be miraculous. Legend has it that the cross was originally erected on a rock where, soon after, a radiant image of a crucified figure was seen on it. Taken to a nearby church, the cross was said to have grown in size. After being moved through a series of churches, the cross was finally placed in the Sé Cathedral in 1845 where it remains till today. The façade of the cathedral originally had two symmetrical towers but the northern one collapsed after being struck by lightening, in 1776. During the Expositions that are held every ten years or so, the sacred relics of St. Francis Xavier are brought from the Basilica of Bom Jesus to the Sé Cathedral for public veneration.

Built by Franciscan Friars over the remains of an older church in 1661, the Church of St. Francis of Assisi has a Tuscan façade with a splendid Manueline-style main doorway. In its time, this church was said to have been the most beautiful in the world. The richly carved and gilded grand altar has an elegantly supported tabernacle. Above is a figure of St. Francis

Goa, in 1873. The gleaming white church looks beautiful not only during the daytime, but even more so at night when the whole structure is illuminated.

Temples

As against temples in other parts of India, Goan temple architecture has been enriched by various influences over the years and exhibits a delightful blend of unique features. Unlike temples elsewhere, here the tower over the main sanctuary is often replaced with a dome. Another distinct feature is the lamp tower (*deepastambh*), usually octagonal in shape and with multiple, beautifully designed windows. Thus, when lit during the temple festivals, the tower is transformed into an impressive pillar of light. The temples also have in their precincts a water tank with steps leading down to the water for pilgrims to perform necessary purification rituals and an elaborate and decorative *tulsi vrindavan*, the receptacle in which the sacred *tulsi* (holy basil) plant is grown. There are myriad beautiful temples all over Goa, but a sizeable number are located in the Ponda area, in the comparatively safe regions that for many years lay outside Portuguese-controlled territory.

The Shri Manguesh Temple at Priol, close to Ponda, is dedicated to Lord Shiva. The image here was smuggled across the river from its original abode at present-day Cortalim during the turbulent days of Portuguese rule. Enter the temple complex and the first thing that catches the eye is the gleaming white, octagonal, seven-storeyed lamp tower. Panels on the bottom storey depict various religious themes. A closer look at the temple reveals domes that sit majestically over the entrance hall, the two side entrances and over the inner sanctum. Around the courtyard are several rooms for pilgrims and an 18th century elegantly designed water tank that is used by the devotees to perform cleansing rituals on festive and auspicious days.

A short distance from the Mangueshi Temple is the Shri Mahalsa Temple at Mardol, with intricately carved pillars at the front. This image was also saved and brought from Verna in the Mormugao Taluka and the temple was constructed in the early 16th century. The main deity is thought to be either a portrayal of Vishnu in the female form or of his consort Laxmi. A special feature of this temple is the unique huge brass pillar that rises from the back of a turtle (an incarnation of Vishnu) with Garuda (the half-eagle half-man mount of

of Assisi embracing Christ on the crucifix whose right arm is lowered and around the shoulders of the saint. The floor of the church is paved with tombstones bearing the names and coat-of-arms of the Portuguese nobility of those days. In the nave on either side of the main altar are paintings in beautiful hues that depict scenes from the life of St. Francis of Assisi. There are several other impressive churches all over Goa, but the Mae de Deus Church at Saligao, located in picturesque village surroundings, is particularly striking due to the stately spires of its Gothic structure. The image here was brought from the ruins of the Mae de Deus Convent at Daugim, Old

Vishnu) perched atop the pillar. The brass lamp is lit during the annual festival of the temple (*zatra*) and on other special festive occasions.

Probably the most popular of all Goa's temples is the Shri Shantadurga Temple at Kavlem, also close to Ponda. In front of the temple stands a six-storeyed lamp tower. This temple was built in 1738, at the behest of Shahu Raja, grandson of the Maratha warrior Shivaji, and is dedicated to the goddess Shantadurga, an incarnation of Parvati, consort of Lord Shiva. Carved wooden doors studded with silver open on to the main entrance hall. Sparkling chandeliers hang from the gilded ceiling and the main shrine with its screen sumptuously worked in silver, houses the deity of Shantadurga flanked on either side by Lord Vishnu and Lord Shiva. The main tower of the temple is topped with a dome while around are red-tiled sloping roofs and walls with ornate arched windows.

The Mahalaxmi Temple at Panjim has an interesting history in that it was the first Hindu temple that was permitted to be built in Goa by the Portuguese, more than 300 years after they conquered Goa. Moved from its original abode at Taleigao to Bicholim in the 16th century fearing destruction by the Portuguese, the deity was again moved, this time to Panjim when the temple was built in 1818.

Above: The beautiful Manguesh Temple at Priol has majestic domes and a seven-storeyed lamp tower. Panels on the bottom storey depict religious themes.

Facing page: The richly gilded main altar at the Basilica of Bom Jesus at Old Goa. The larger image with upraised arm is that of St. Ignatius of Loyola; below is the smaller figure of the Infant Jesus.

Previous page: The Shantadurga temple at Kavlem, probably the most popular of all Goa's temples, has a dome over the main tower, red-tiled sloping roofs and ornate arched windows.

Following page: Goa is endowed with several magnificent Churches that are a delightful blend of European and Indian craftsmanship.

Page 57: The Sé Cathedral opposite the Basilica of Bom Jesus at Old Goa.

The small temple of Shri Saptakoteshwar at Narve is dedicated to Lord Saptakoteshwara, the much-favoured patron and family deity of the Kadambas. The deity was originally installed in a temple on the island of Diwar, but when Goa fell to the Muslims, devotees buried it in a rice field fearing defilement. It was later found and subsequent to the Portuguese persecution it was moved to its present site at Narve. During an attempt to oust the Portuguese, Shivaji paid a visit to this temple and ordered its renovation in 1688. More recently, the Fundação Oriente has provided funds for its renovation.

One of Goa's oldest existing temples, located deep in the forested interiors at Tambdi Surla a few kilometres from Mollem, is also most unusual. This is the only intact surviving temple of the Kadamba era and its remote location was probably the reason that it escaped destruction by both the Muslims and the Portuguese. Dedicated to Shri Mahadeva, it is believed to have been built during the 11th-13th century. It is built of black basalt stone, which itself is unusual for this region, where laterite was the material chiefly used. Stark black with chiselled carvings, the temple makes an exquisite picture as it stands in sharp contrast to the lush greenery around. Even more remarkable is that it has been built by skillfully fitting stone into stone, with no indication of any mortar having been used. Set on a low plinth, the temple faces east with its main hall accessible from three sides via steps around the front. The hall has ten pillars and the turret above the sanctum has miniature relief and fine carvings of Brahma, Vishnu, Shiva and Parvati.

Mosques

There are many mosques all over Goa, though most are of comparatively recent origin. During the last years of Bijapuri

The story of St. Francis Xavier, affectionately called *Goencho Saib*, is fascinating indeed. Born in Spain in 1506, Francis was yet a young boy when his family lost all their property as a consequence of the annexation of Navarre by King Fernando of Aragon. Leaving for Paris to pursue his studies, young Francis began to lead a dissolute student life. Thankfully he soon met Ignatius de Loyola, under whose influence he changed completely. From a profligate young lad, Francis became devoutly religious and was subsequently ordained to priesthood. When a companion deputed to the colonies fell ill Francis was sent instead, and in 1542 he arrived in Goa. Tending to the sick and the lepers, Francis also began teaching catechism. It is said that he would walk the streets ringing a little brass bell to draw the crowds. His novel way of teaching attracted many, particularly as he often sang the lessons to make them more enjoyable and easier to learn.

After his first short sojourn in Goa, Francis made journeys to other parts of India and the East, and though he returned several times it was never for extended periods. In 1552, he left on a voyage to China. Landing on the island of Sancian, he fell seriously ill, and on 3rd December 1552, he passed away. He was buried and his body packed around with lime to hasten its decomposition. In 1553, the gravesite was dug up to transport the remains to Malacca and onward to Goa. To everyone's surprise the body was found to be fresh as if he had just passed away. Taken to Malacca, it was reburied and five months later was again exhumed and brought by ship to Goa in March 1554. It was a touching return as church bells rang and guns boomed with hundreds of people gathering at the quayside to have a look at the life-like body. Over the centuries, constant exposure led to the partial drying and desiccation of the body. It was therefore decided to enclose it within a crystal glass casket, now housed within a silver reliquary in the Basilica of Bom Jesus. Francis was canonized as a saint in 1622, with innumerable miracles being attributed to him. The exposition of the sacred relics is now held every ten years, the last one having been held in 2004.

rule, there were several mosques built around the Ponda area, which were subsequently destroyed by the Portuguese. However, the Safa Shahouri Masjid, built by Adil Shah in 1560, still survives. This mosque is unusual in that it does not exhibit the traditional Muslim architecture with minarets, but has a rectangular prayer hall with window arches and a slanting tiled roof. There is also a sacred tank with intricate designs adjacent to the mosque. Lavish gardens and sparkling fountains once surrounded the mosque, and though no longer there the peaceful surroundings lend an air of tranquil serenity.

Traditional Goan Homes

Yet another enchanting aspect of Goa is its unique architectural style, nowhere expressed as delightfully as in its old-world houses which exhibit an exquisite blend of Eastern and Western features. Some houses are huge and imposing, others more modest dwellings, and yet all have an undeniable kind of charm about them. As you wind your way along roads that gently snake through sleepy villages, charming facades of these houses catch your eye and your imagination, making you wonder about the people who live there. Turn around a corner and it's very likely that you might see a mass of bougainvillea spilling over a freshly painted compound wall, branches weighed down by brightly coloured blooms. Peer through and you might spot a house bathed in sunlight, its red-tiled roof and its ornate verandah with trellised railings creating a picture-postcard sight that looks ever so cosy and inviting. Or you could chance upon a compound wall with a wrought iron gate flanked on either side by a pillar, atop which sits an impassive stone lion, one paw majestically upraised. Beyond, a long flight of steps leads up to a huge imposing mansion whose weathered exterior, shuttered windows and closed doors give it an intriguing air of mystery. Goa's houses, especially the grand mansions built by the aristocratic gentry of yesteryear, exude a fascinating old-world charm evocative of a bygone era.

Above: One of Goa's best known magnificient old homes is the Braganza Mansion at Chandor, whose beautiful front facade has many bay windows overlooking a pretty garden.

Facing page, top: Unique gateposts are seen outside many Goan homes with figures of lions, dogs, cocks and even saluting soldiers placed atop.

Facing page, bottom, left: Curtains frame the window as sunlight streams in, accentrating the pretty design of the window.

Facing page, bottom, right: Typical interior of a drawing room in a Christian home with a crucifix on the wall.

Evolution of the Goan House

Goan domestic architecture evolved over time, a result of inherent conditions and of outside influences. As renowned architect Gerard da Cunha explains, "Factors like local availability of materials as well as climatic conditions played an important part in the evolution of the Goan home. I think Goa was very generous to its house-builder. We had easily available building material like laterite stone that was soft enough to be cut and utilized. We also had thatch and wood from our trees, and shell lime from our estuarine waters. The form of the houses was dependent on climatic conditions as well. In a place like Goa where we have heavy rainfall, sloping roofs allowed for proper drainage. Then again, with a warm and humid climate like ours, airy courtyards provided ample ventilation. The height of the plinth was also raised so as to guard against dampness. Of course, later on there were other factors like the Portuguese influence and changes in lifestyle. With a grander lifestyle, the form of the house also became more elaborate. Bigger rooms were built, and courtyards became larger too. The front porch or *balcao* was then introduced and people, especially womenfolk who had rarely ventured out earlier, could now sit down for an evening chat with the neighbours. Other functional and decorative influences followed, like the Italian or Roman influence in the form of columns, windows, arches and flooring."

Traditional Goan homes in the pre-Portuguese days were most likely built around a main courtyard having the *tulsi* (holy basil) at its centre and a common verandah running along its inner fringe. The front portion of the quadrangle would have been a reception area for guests, the portion at the rear would have housed the kitchen and dining areas, while the rooms at the side would likely have been the living quarters. Of course, then as now, houses were constructed according to economic status, where a humble householder would have had a much simpler dwelling place, his home probably constructed with plain mud walls and thatched roof.

And yet all houses, from the grandest mansions to the simplest village homes, had their own distinctive character and appeal. The different succession of rulers over the ages also played a part in influencing the changing styles of art and architecture. The arrival of the Portuguese and subsequent conversions to Christianity had their own impact, where the neo-convert adopted new elements of style in his domestic architecture. Yet, the Goan Christian, while assuming an outwardly Westernized sensibility, still clung to much of his earlier ethnic traditions and customs. These found expression particularly in the inner spaces of his home where basic interior designs often remained similar, albeit with some changes. The arrangement of a central courtyard along with the internal connecting verandah often continued, while the family chapel or altar seen even today in many old stately homes was probably a modification of the traditional Hindu *puja* area. Many Hindu merchants and aristocrats, particularly those who had business or official dealings with the Portuguese also adopted some Western features in their homes, especially in the reception area for guests. The in-built stone seats seen in many a *balcao*, along with its characteristic pyramidal tiled roof, are a unique feature seen in many Goan homes. An example of creativity

and innovation in using locally available materials is apparent in the ingenious manner in which windows were covered before glass became available. The translucent mother-of-pearl from large shells found in Goa's riverine estuaries was trimmed into squares, polished and fitted into a wooden framework to make quaint window shutters. In fact, even today, this kind of shutter can still be seen on the windows of several old houses all over the state. Ornate furniture crafted by the Goan artisan also exhibited themes reflective of his earlier traditions and ethos where older traditional designs were often skillfully interspersed with the newer European motifs. As lifestyles became grander, so did the interiors and exteriors. Large windows and slender pillars were incorporated which gave an appearance of light, delicacy and elegance. Opulent furnishings adorned the interiors, coloured materials were imaginatively used to produce exquisite patterns on the flooring, while stucco mouldings in different designs became popular over doors and window frames.

Magnificent Mansions

There are several stately homes all across Goa that were built centuries ago and which provide a fascinating glimpse at not only the architecture, but also the elegant lifestyle of those

days. A few of these are the Loyola Furtado house at Chinchinim, the Miranda Mansion at Loutolim (belonging to Goa's famed cartoonist and illustrator, Mario Miranda), the Inacio da Silva House at Margao, the Godinho Jacques house at Majorda and the Deshprabhu House at Pernem. Each of these grand mansions is distinctive in its own way. Take for example, the palatial Deshprabhu ancestral home at Pernem which is probably the only one in Goa that features a gate-house. Incidentally, the Deshprabhu family is unique in another respect as well in that the title of Viscount was conferred by the Portuguese to the head of the family in 1882. The Inacio da Silva House at Margao is an imposing mansion also known as the 'House of Seven Gables' or *Sat Burnzam Ghor* referring to the original seven pyramidal crests on its roof of which only three remain now.

Possibly one of the grandest of all Goa's stately homes is the Braganza Mansion at Chandor, in South Goa. Built in the 16th century by the wealthy Braganza family, the exterior of this grand edifice reveals a striking façade that has over two

dozen bay windows overlooking a pretty garden. Two branches of the family now occupy the mansion – the Braganza Pereira family live in the east wing of the house, while the west wing is occupied by the Menezes Braganza family. Famed journalist and fiery exponent of the freedom movement, Luis de Menezes Braganza was one of the more illustrious descendants of the Menezes Braganza branch. Forced due to their political views to flee from Chandor in 1950, the Menezes Braganza family returned in 1962 to find their house almost completely intact having been taken care of during the interim period by just one faithful family retainer. The mansion is sumptuously furnished with ornately carved furniture in rosewood and ebony, rare Chinese and Japanese jars, plates and crockery, a fine silver collection and several other objects d'art. The private library holds a fine collection of over 1500 books that were assiduously collected by Luis de Menezes Braganza. Sparkling Belgium chandeliers hang from the ceiling of the huge ballroom while paintings and large gilded mirrors adorn the walls. In the east wing, several palanquins (*machilas*) stand in the long inner verandah, while a sacred relic in the form of a diamond encrusted nail of St. Francis Xavier lies enshrined in the family chapel.

Not too far from the Braganza Mansion is another heritage

home which is also open to the public. This is the Casa Grande (also known as *Voddlem Ghor*) located near the St. James Chapel at Chandor. Owned by Sara Fernandes, this house has several very interesting historical artifacts and objects on display, many dating back centuries. Sara explains that "the house was built in pre-Portuguese times and is more than 500 years old, with some additions made in phases around 250 years ago." The huge halls have beautifully carved furniture with Indian and European motifs, chandeliers from Belgium, and an exquisite porcelain collection including plates and crockery sets from Macau. Finely carved four poster beds, complete with fabric canopies, occupy the bedrooms. There are several other interesting objects like wooden cabinets with secret compartments, and documents written in the ancient Indian Modi script. The family is proud of the Hindu ancestry of past generations, and Sara points to a palanquin used in pre-Portuguese times which was used, she tells us, "to transport the family *bhat* (Hindu priest) who was comfortably seated on pillows within." But the most unusual feature in this house is a cleverly disguised underground passage that leads to the nearby river. As Sara's youngest son Ranjeev leads us down the steps and through this passage, he points out several large holes which he explains were 'gun holes' and it is easy to imagine how these were designed to keep a hostile enemy at bay. While there is no fixed fee to view these houses, both the Braganza Mansion as well as Casa Grande have wooden boxes discreetly placed for donations, the proceeds going towards the maintenance of the house.

Apart from ancestral homes that are being maintained by family members or caretakers, there are scores of others that are in a neglected state as their owners have either migrated elsewhere or are not able to maintain them. Consequently, these homes often crumble or fall to the builder's axe, when they are mercilessly torn down to make way for huge unimaginative building complexes, a far cry from their earlier grandeur. Perhaps the government should step in with some sort of viable plans for their restoration and upkeep, to ensure that the important cultural heritage represented by these houses is not lost forever. Fortunately, an increasing number of owners have realized the historical importance of their homes and are not only restoring them, but also allow viewing to interested visitors, thus giving one a chance to learn about and appreciate the antiquity and architectural significance of these grand old Goan mansions.

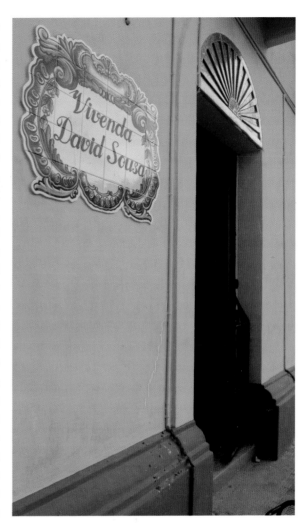

Above: Hand painted azulejos ceramic tiles are often used for the nameplate outside the front door of a Goan home.

Facing page: Creativity and innovation in using locally available materials is apparent in the ingenious manner in which windows were covered before glass became available. The translucent mother-of-pearl was trimmed into squares, polished and fitted into a wooden framework to make quaint window shutters.

Previous page, left: In the east wing of the Braganza Mansion at Chandor, several palanquins (machilas) stand in the long inner verandah.

Previous page, right: One of the facades of the Braganza Mansion.

Page 62: A prettily designed staircase adds to the beauty and elegance of this Goan home.

Page 66: Typically, small balconies like this one provide a functional as well as a decorative element that further enhances the beauty of the window.

Page 67: Ornately carved furniture, sparkling lights from chandeliers and wall sconces, and beautifully designed arched windows add to the grandeur of the reception halls.

Anyone with an interest in Goan homes would probably find a trip to Gerard da Cunha's delightful museum 'Houses of Goa' well worth a visit. Winner of several awards and rated amongst the best architects in the country, Gerard has set up the museum as an interesting chronicle of the rich architectural and historical aspects of Goan domestic architecture. Located in the sleepy village of Torda, the museum is just a short drive down from the O'Coqueiro junction at Porvorim. Built in exposed laterite, it is a three-storeyed structure designed in the unusual shape of a ship. Inside, coloured photographic mounts of some of Goa's famed houses allow you to have a closer look at the salient features of each house. Models and plans of individual houses show exact locations of *balcao*, verandah, lobby, library, living room, bedrooms and prayer rooms. A set of panels gives more detailed information about the elements of style of floorings, false ceilings, staircases, bedrooms, courtyards, kitchens, wells and compound walls in the old Goan houses. There are also replicas of columns, eavesboards, railings, altars, etc from different houses, which show the actual building materials used and allow you to examine each in greater detail. The museum has been described as a resource-cum-research centre for the traditional architecture of Goa.

Culinary Delights

Goan cuisine is best described as an exuberant fusion of food and flavour that bears the stamp of Hindu, Muslim and Christian influences, where each religious community also has its own distinct fare. The cuisine of the Goan Christian tends more towards the non-vegetarian and exhibits more of the Portuguese influence than that of the Goan Hindu, which includes a far greater variety of vegetarian fare. As a whole, however, Goan cuisine offers you a tantalizing culinary experience, the remembrance of which lingers long after you have sampled it, leaving you with a hankering for more.

Above: Raw mango pickle makes a delightful accompaniment to any meal.

Top: A variety of fruits are available in the local markets.

Right: Tiny but potent-piri-piri chilly.

Outside Influences

Goan cuisine was undoubtedly influenced over the years by the various cultures that the region came in contact with. During the long years of Portuguese rule, many traditional food habits were modified and new ones embraced, some by choice, others by enforcement through edicts and decrees. Chillies, now an indispensable part of local cuisine, were first introduced to India by the Portuguese as were other items like potatoes, tomatoes, pineapples, papayas, cashews, etc. The Portuguese introduced the practice of eating meat to the converts, and this gradually became a regular part of the Christian diet. Many a time, original recipes were adapted making use of locally available ingredients or changes incorporated to suit local palates and these became distinctive dishes in themselves. The use of vinegar in Goan Catholic cuisine was another legacy of the Portuguese; Goan Hindus traditionally use sour lime, tamarind or *kokum* to impart sourness to a dish. Cashew nuts, now extremely sought-after and a favourite takeaway item from Goa, were unknown earlier. It was Portuguese traders who first introduced the cashew tree from Brazil in South America. Oven-baked bread, now popular with Goans from all communities, was also a result of Western influence. Yet, the culinary exchange was not merely a one-way affair. Many items, most notably exotic spices from various parts of India, including Goa, made their way across the seas, lending their distinctive flavour to many a Western dish.

Above: A typical Goan meal of fish, curry and rice.

Top: A variety of fresh fish on sale in the local market.

Fish, Curry and Rice

Goa's proximity to the sea ensures a generous supply of fresh seafood. Not surprisingly, therefore, fish is close to the Goan heart, and the common man savours his staple diet of fish, curry and rice. In Goa, fish is more than just an item on the menu. It is something of more importance, so much so that when acquaintances meet, a common question smilingly asked is, *"Aiz koslem nustem ghetlam?"* which translates as, "What fish have you bought today?" Buying, preparing and eating fish is part of the daily routine. The fish markets are bustling places where the vendors, mostly womenfolk, sit with their wares of fish laid out invitingly in front of them. There is a wide array and choice of seafood – pomfret, mackerels, sardines, shark, herring, mullet, sole, squid, kingfish, crabs, mussels and prawns are just some of the varieties available. And as everyone looks for the freshest fish and the best bargains, the sounds of good-natured haggling can be heard everywhere.

After the fish has been selected and bought, it is time to cook it. Ingredients that go into the mouthwatering curries of Goa generally include coconut, garlic, turmeric, dry coriander, red chillies, pepper, cumin and tamarind, ground together into a fine paste. Although modern conveniences are now used in urban areas and in small households, the traditional way of cooking on firewood in vessels of fired clay, using wooden *doules* (spoons) made of coconut shells, still continues in most rural areas. The curry is allowed to simmer on a slow fire till it thickens, the choice of fish is added and it is then cooked for a short while more to make a tantalizingly spicy preparation that goes well with steaming hot rice. Many Goans, especially in rural areas, still prefer to eat the local

Above: Goans savour their staple diet of fish that is more than just an item on the menu.

Facing page: Treat for the taste buds - a vendor holds out a string of the spicy Goan sausage or chouris.

Following page, top: Growing in abundance during the season, jackfruit is either eaten as a table fruit or is made into preserves like the much sought-after jackfruit 'Sattam'.

Following page, bottom: When fully ripened, locally grown pineapples are sweet, juicy and have a most delectable taste.

parboiled rice, called *ukdo tandul*, preferably the unpolished red-streaked variety that is considered more nutritious.

There are several other types of curries including *ambot-tik* which is a reddish curry with a hot and sour tang and made without coconut, the delectable mackerel *uddamethi* made mostly in Hindu households and crab *xec xec*, a dish of crab cooked in spicy coconut gravy. Eating fish is not limited to curried preparations alone. Fish fried with a light dusting of semolina mixed with powdered spices is the usual tasty, everyday fare. There is a variety of other fish dishes as well

– fish *recheiado* (a tasty preparation of fried fish stuffed with a paste of red chillies and other spices ground in vinegar), delicious *masala* fried prawns, *tisreo sukem* (a dry preparation of clams cooked in their shells in a spicy coconut *masala)*, dry prawn *kismur* (a savoury accompaniment made from dry prawns with coconut, chillies and onion) – the list is endless. Then there are pickled seafood dishes too, like the tangy fish or prawn *balchao, parra* and *molho* preparations. These are also available commercially in convenient packs which visitors often carry with them when leaving, hoping to relish a little bit of the taste of Goan seafood and rekindle fond memories even when far away.

The Local Pao

Live anywhere in Goa and it is almost certain that you will be awakened to a unique sound every morning, a repetitive honking that alerts the neighbourhood to the arrival of the *poder*. The Konkani word *poder*, probably derived from the Portuguese word 'padeiro' is loosely used for both a baker as

well as the baker's delivery boy. Warm, fragrant and oven-fresh, Goa's delicious local bread is an essential item in many households for breakfast or dinner. It goes well with morning coffee or tea and is the perfect accompaniment to spicy gravy dishes too. The *poder*, who generally goes around in the morning and evening, carries a wide variety of bread in a large, cloth-covered cane basket strapped to the back of his bicycle. Even during the heavy rains of the monsoon season or on chilly December mornings, he still faithfully makes his rounds. When oven-baked bread was first introduced in Goa centuries ago, toddy was used to leaven it, though nowadays yeast is more often used for the purpose. There are several different types of bread including the *pao*, a small square bread, the bow-shaped *katre pao*, the *pokshie* with slits in the top crust, the *kankon* (bangle), a crisp large ring-shaped bread that is usually dunked in one's tea and eaten, the *gutli*, a longish roll of bread, the *khadak* pao, a deliciously crusty bread with a soft inside and the *poie*, a brown bread said to have a high fibre content and good for diabetics. The *poie* being somewhat hollow inside, one can slit it open and stuff it with either potato *bhaji*, the spicy *chouris* or some such filling to make a tasty snack. Despite the fact that commercial sliced bread is now easily available and that innovative

Above: Goan markets stock varieties of fruit produced locally and from neighbouring states.

Previous page, top left: Different Goan breads including the pao, *the* poie, *the* katre pao *and the* kankon.

Previous page, top right: A dish of the tasty halsandeachem tonnak (butter beans in gravy).

Previous page, centre left: Tempting tiger prawns in a bed of fresh salad.

Previous page, centre right: Bebinca is a rich, almost sinfully delicious multi-layered concoction that practically melts in the mouth as you eat it.

Previous page, bottom: A variety of locally grown vegetables is available at all markets.

varieties have been introduced in several resorts and in coastal areas, especially in North Goa, it is obvious that with so many diehard fans the delicious Goan *pao* is here to stay. Truly, the Goan *poder* has become something of an institution, a familiar fixture as it were, that has survived changing times.

Fruits and Vegetables

Several fruits and vegetables are grown locally and the markets, especially in the towns, usually stock the local varieties as well as produce that come in from the neighbouring states.

Locally grown vegetables include pumpkins (*dudhi*), radish (*mulo*), brinjals (*vaingin*), cucumber (*toushim*), long beans (*val*), cluster beans (*chidki-midki*), ridged gourd (*ghosalim*), ash gourd (*kunvalo*), bottle gourd (*konkan dudhi*), and okra or lady fingers (*bhendi*). Locally grown fruits include bananas, papayas, mangoes, pineapples, *chikoos*, pomegranates, watermelons and jackfruits.

Typical and Festive Fare

But while the seafood in Goa is legendary, the sheer variety of delectable dishes of all kinds, from soups and starters to main dishes and desserts, makes the cuisine nothing short of a gourmet's delight. If you are fortunate enough to be invited to a Goan home for a meal, don't miss out on the opportunity. Almost any occasion, from a birthday celebration to an elaborate wedding buffet is a chance to indulge in a veritable feast as it were. Typical starters in a Catholic household might include *rissois de camarao* (tiny prawn puffs), croquettes (small, spicy, fried meat rolls) or *empadinhas* (small pork pies). The soups that follow could be *caldo verde* (a light spinach and potato soup) or *sopa grossa* (a thicker broth with vegetables and meat). Popular main dishes include pork *vindalho* (chunks of pork cooked in a pungent red gravy), chicken *cafreal* (chicken pieces marinated in a green chilly-ginger-garlic paste and fried) and Goa's famous *sarapatel* or *sorpotel* (diced and fried pork oddments cooked in a spicy red gravy) which is often served with *sannam* (soft rice cakes leavened with toddy). Steaming hot rice is served, either plain white and fluffy or in the form of a *pulao*. Another treat for the taste buds is the tempting Goan *chouriço* or *chouris*, a spicy pork sausage eaten either as a dish by itself or with the addition perhaps of potatoes and onions. *Chouris* is also added to enhance the taste of other dishes as in *feijoada* (a dish of beans spiced with sausage). The enticing *khatkhatem* (a delicious gravy dish

made from diced vegetables, roots and fruits in season) and *halsandeachem tonnak* (butter beans in gravy) are commonly served in most Hindu homes. Chicken *xacuti* (chicken pieces cooked in a rich gravy of coconut and roasted spices) is very popular in both Catholic and Hindu households, though the methods of cooking differ slightly. And, the most popular Muslim contribution to Goan cuisine is the mouthwatering *biryani*, its aroma wafting temptingly through the neighbourhood, especially at festival time. *Sol kaddi*, a refreshing drink made from the skins of the dried *kokum* fruit serves as a digestive, and is generally drunk at the end of a meal in Hindu households.

There are several delightful desserts to follow the main meal such as caramel custard and *pais* (a rice *kheer*). However, many consider *bebinca* as the ultimate delicacy, the crowning glory as it were, of a delicious meal. *Bebinca* is a rich, multi-layered pudding made from egg yolks, coconut milk, sugar and flour and is served in thin slices. When baked slowly, layer by layer and prepared in the traditional way by an expert, the end result is a rich, almost sinfully delicious concoction that practically melts in the mouth as you eat it.

Different foods are prepared for different occasions and according to the various festivals, rituals and the availability of particular items in season. Thus, you have a variety of traditional items, both savoury and sweet, made during Ganesh Chaturthi, one of the important Hindu festivals in Goa. Steamed *modaks*, different varieties of *ladoos*, *fenoreo*, coconut *kapam* and *nevreos* are only some of the many sweets made during that time. Hindus celebrate the festival of Nagapanchami and Catholics the feast of the Assumption,

with deliciously fragrant *pattoleos*, little parcels of jaggery and coconut enclosed in rice paste and steamed in turmeric leaves. Diwali is celebrated with different dishes of *faw* (beaten rice) amongst other items. During Id festivities, Muslims traditionally prepare sweet dishes like *sheer kurma*, *sevyan ka zardaa* or *firni*. And, at Christmas there is a wide array of sweets, from *doce de grao* (a gram and coconut sweet), *dodol* (a dark rice halwa) and *batica* (semolina cake) to *bolinhas*, *nevreos* and rich Christmas fruit cake.

Goa's Famed Drink - Feni !

Both alcoholic and non-alcoholic drinks are available aplenty in Goa, but it is undoubtedly the local brew, *feni,* that is Goa's most well-known alcoholic beverage. There are two varieties of *feni*, coconut or palm *feni* and cashew *feni,* each with its own characteristic aroma, flavour and taste. Unlike coconut *feni*, which is produced throughout the year, the production of cashew *feni* is seasonal as the cashew apple from which it is made is available only around March to late May. Coconut *feni* is prepared from the fresh sap or toddy collected morning or evening from coconut trees by local toddy tappers who shin up the tree trunks with practiced ease. Fresh toddy is non-alcoholic and at this stage makes a refreshing, somewhat sweetish, drink with a characteristic taste, but within a few hours it begins to naturally ferment. This fermented liquid is then distilled in a still to obtain coconut *feni*. In traditional local stills the liquid is kept in a large pot of fired clay or copper under which burns a wood fire. The hot vapours exit through a tube passing through a tank filled with cool water, and the distillate that condenses is then collected in suitable containers.

Above: Traditional vessels at Casa Grande, Chandor. Water remains cool in the terracotta pot (gurgurette)and is poured through the beak of the rooster which also doubles up as a decorative spout.

Top: Beach side shacks offer a variety of delicious food and drink.

Facing page: Lunch at a spice farm is a treat, laid out in earthern ware dishes and eaten on banana leaves placed on bamboo platters.

Previous page: Goa's famed drink 'Feni' often comes in innovative packaging, making for attractive gifts or souvenirs to take back home.

Cashew *feni* is produced from the cashew fruit or cashew apple as it is called. (Technically, the cashew apple is a pseudo-fruit since it is actually a swollen stalk or peduncle, but in common parlance it is referred to as the fruit.) Around March-April, the aroma of the ripening fruit, especially on the hillsides where there are often large plantations, signals that the cashew season has arrived. Often, one can also get the heady whiff of the ongoing *feni* distillation process. Cashew apples are seen practically all over the countryside, plump orange-yellow or reddish-yellow fruits with a solitary nut growing on the outside and hanging below the apple. Cashew *feni* is obtained by distilling the juice got by crushing the ripe fruit after first removing the nut. Earlier, the fruits were crushed underfoot, but nowadays mechanical crushers are increasingly being used to extract the juice. This juice called *neera*, also makes for a very refreshing drink when fresh. The juice is allowed to ferment and then distilled, the first distillate being the somewhat light *urrak*. A proportion of this *urrak* is added to the fermented *neera* and re-distilled to get the stronger and more potent cashew *feni*.

Urrak can be drunk as soon as it is distilled and in fact, is considered to be an extremely pleasant summer drink especially when mixed with lemon juice and soda. While

The luscious golden mango, known as the 'King of fruits', is undoubtedly Goa's most beloved and best known fruit. Originally known by the Tamil word '*mang-kay*,' the name was thought to have been corrupted to '*manga*' by the Portuguese when they came to India, and from this the present word 'mango' was derived. More interesting still is the fact that several Goan varieties of mangoes seem to have been baptized with Portuguese names and thus you have mangoes with quaint names like *Afonso, Fernandine, Xavier* and *Colaço*! Undoubtedly, the best of all the varieties though, are Goa's famed *Mancurad* or *Malcorada* mangoes. Premium *Malcorada* mangoes with their smooth, delicate flesh have a sweet delectable taste that is arguably unparalleled by any other variety. Not surprisingly they are also the most costly of all varieties. Raw mangoes are used in several preparations like pickles and preserves, while ripe mangoes, apart from being eaten as table fruit, are also converted into various products like jams and squashes.

cashew *feni*, with its distinctive aroma, character and flavour, has been compared to Mexico's famed tequila, it has also been called 'the local firewater' and not without reason. Both *urrak* and *feni* can appear deceptively mild with the real 'kick' hitting you only after a while. *Feni* tastes better when matured, when it develops a more mellow flavour and taste. It can be had in small quantities as an aperitif or used as a base for cocktails. Traditionally, it also has a medicinal value and is used in small quantities for the treatment of chest colds and several other ailments. Sometimes *feni* is mixed with other spirits, so if you plan to sample this local brew do ask around and make sure that you get the genuine drink from a reliable source. Nowadays, *feni* is also available in bottles of various shapes and sizes, which make attractive gifts or even souvenirs to take back home.

Eating Out

If you've missed out on an invitation to a local home for the taste of a real Goan home-cooked meal don't be disheartened. There are scores of restaurants ranging from tiny little places to chic joints, which serve excellent Goan cuisine. A few popular ones are Martin's Corner at Betalbatim, Longuinhos at Margao, Chef Fernando's Nostalgia in the village of Raia close to Margao, Venite Restaurant at Panjim, Martin's Beach Corner at Caranzalem, Souza-Lobo's at Calangute and O'Coqueiro at Porvorim. (Incidentally, the notorious international criminal Charles Sobhraj was nabbed while dining at the O'Coqueiro restaurant in 1986, soon after his escape from a Delhi jail.) Many beachside shacks also serve very good Goan food, though with some of the newer ones that have employed non-Goan cooks, authenticity is sometimes a question. Besides Goan food, many restaurants serve North Indian and South Indian specialties and Continental fare as well.

Festive Goa

Festivals are an integral part of life in Goa, and their vibrancy and colour are a vivid reflection of Goa's rich cultural inheritance. While most festivals are a celebration of religious events, others relate to the changing seasons and harvests. Still others are a legacy of enduring, age-old tribal customs. Not only do festivals enliven Goa's social life, but they also serve to cement the bonds between the different communities, uniting them in a joyous commemoration of memorable events and shared memories of a common past. Goans have always been tolerant of each other's beliefs and despite few attempts for petty political gains to disrupt the harmony, they still continue to live in a peaceful state of co-existence. Apart from the main important festivals, each village or town usually celebrates a distinct religious festival or *zatra* of its own to which fascinating legends and customs are often associated.

Above: A handshake with smilling clowns at the carnival float parade.
Facing page: King Momo and his entourage lead the float parade.

Custom and Tradition

One of the nicer aspects of the celebrations of festivals like Diwali, Id, Ganesh Chaturthi and Christmas is the exchange of festive food and sweets between neighbours and friends, irrespective of religion. Customs such as these serve to strengthen the bonds between communities and enrich societal links. At most religious festivals, colourful, bustling fairs spring up close to the churches or temples where the festival is being celebrated. All kinds of articles are sold at the fairs and vendors too move around in the crowd with items like balloons and small toys. There are usually several stalls with heaps of roasted gram and all kinds of sweets. A favourite item is *kaddio-boddio* (also known as *khajem*),

delicious sticks made of chickpea flour which are fried and then coated in either jaggery or sugar. Close to the churches and temples, one can purchase traditional items to be offered to the deity like garlands of fresh marigolds, candles, bananas and coconuts. Another common sight at several fairs is that of vendors selling small wax replicas of different parts of the body like arms, legs, eyes, ears, etc. There is a quaint custom where devotees buy and offer these replicas to the deity at the shrine, in the belief that they will be cured from whatever ailments they suffer from in that particular part of the body. At some of the larger fairs, household utensils and wooden furniture are also on sale. Scarcely a week goes by without a festival being celebrated in some part or the other, and a glimpse at just a few of these offers an interesting insight into some festive traditions of Goa.

Through the Year

The festive spirit begins early in the year with the Feast of the Three Kings, which commemorates the visit of the three

Above and facing page: An artistically designed float at the carnival parade depicting fish amongst swirling waves.

Wise Men to the newly born baby Jesus at Bethlehem. Celebrated on the 6th of January in the three villages of Reis Magos, Cansaulim and Chandor, the event at all three places is marked with much fanfare, pomp and pageantry. Dressed in resplendent royal finery and each accompanied by their own entourage, the three young boys are crowned as kings. Bearing gifts, the boys travel on horseback up to the church for the Feast Mass and other rituals. Later, a litany is held at the house of each boy, following which relatives and friends are treated to a grand repast.

The annual festival of Shantadurga at Fatorpa is a momentous affair with devotees coming from all over for the traditional rituals and festivities. The festival is also celebrated with great fervour at the Shantadurga temple in the village of Kavlem where the deity is taken around in procession with much pomp and grandeur. There is an interesting observance associated with the Fatorpa temple. During the Portuguese era, the deity was secretly transferred here from the village of Cuncolim due to apprehensions that it might be destroyed. Nowadays, a unique procession called the Sontreo Festival or Festival of Umbrellas is held during the month of Phalguna when Shantadurga is ceremoniously taken to her original abode at Cuncolim. Twelve umbrellas represent the twelve clans of Cuncolim. Christians as well as Hindus take part in this colourful procession in acknowledgement of original ancestral rights, going back to the days when five of the original twelve Hindu clans representing the village were constrained to embrace Christianity.

A few days before Lent, Goa celebrates the Carnival, considered to be a period of merriment before the austere days that follow. There is, however, no direct religious significance attached to this festival. From earlier times when the festivities were spontaneous, the government now organizes parades in all the major towns, making it a somewhat contrived affair. Nevertheless, there is an air of gaiety and excited anticipation especially amongst the tourists, and the bonhomie is infectious as large crowds line the streets to watch the colourfully decorated float parades with

Above: Traditional folk dances at the Shigmo parade.

Facing page: The Lamp dance where the performer skillfully balances brass lamps while performing intricate dance movements.

Following page: Colourful participants at the Carnival parade.

Page 89, top: Stalls selling the tempting 'Kaddio - boddio (Khajem)' and other sweets are a typical sight at local fairs.

Page 89, bottom: Blessing of the new harvest after the monsoons isa common sight all over Goa.

participants in fancy costumes. King Momo, the mock king of revelry, leads the pageant along with his retinue, all attired in full costume. To the delight of the crowds, King Momo winds up the parade by reading aloud a jocular proclamation, exhorting his subjects to enjoy three days of merrymaking. Shigmo, the Goan counterpart of the Holi festival celebrated in the rest of the country, welcomes the arrival of spring with much rejoicing and gaiety. Men and young lads sprinkle colour on each other, the bright colours symbolizing the vibrant hues of spring. Even those who are initially not too keen on the exchange of colour, often find themselves caught up in the fervour and join in with much enthusiasm. Government-

sponsored float parades, on similar lines as the Carnival parades, are organized in most towns. The mood is exuberant and the air is filled with the echo of drums, cymbals and chanting as traditional dancers in colourful costumes move in rhythmic step. The huge floats that follow bring religious mythology alive in an artistic display of light, colour and sound effects.

There are several local celebrations around this time in many villages all over Goa. The Zambaulim Shigmo is celebrated at the Damodar Temple at Zambaulim, where males exchange colour in a spree of riotous revelry before bathing themselves in the river close by. There are also a few local festivals where unusual tribal rituals are performed which have been carried down from ancient times. One such is the Shisharanni festival celebrated at the centuries-old Mallikarjun temple at Shristal, in Canacona. One of the rituals involves the passing of a needle and thread through the superficial skin on the backs of newly married men. Another ritual has three holy men lying prostrate on the ground with their turbaned heads close together in a semi-circle in the centre. A pot of rice is placed on their heads and a small fire is lit underneath in the small space between their heads to cook the rice. It may sound quite incredible, yet having witnessed it myself, I can attest that this unusual ritual does indeed take place. The rice cooked in the pot is later sprinkled on the devotees as a blessing from the gods. The festival is celebrated every alternate year and, the last ceremony having been held in March 2007, the next festival should take place during the Shigmo celebrations in 2009. Incidentally, the Mallikarjun temple is also popular with devotees seeking advice from the oracles.

During the Lenten season, on the Monday prior to Palm Sunday, there is the unique Procession of Saints at St. Andrew's Church, in Goa Velha. In a centuries-old tradition, around 26 life-size statues of different saints belonging to the Third Order of the Franciscans are carried on palanquins in a grand procession that winds its way along the main thoroughfare accompanied by hundreds of devotees. A couple of weeks later, the sombre days of Lent come to an end with the celebration of Easter, commemorating the resurrection of Jesus. Midnight Masses are held in many churches all over the state, and children enjoy the chocolate Easter eggs that are often part of the customary festive fare.

Id-ul-Fitr is the Muslim festival that marks the end of the Ramadan period of fasting. Id prayers are recited, relatives and friends joyously greet each other and special festive delicacies like *sheer kurma* are prepared.

A fortnight after Easter comes the Milagres *Fest*, the feast of Our Lady of Miracles celebrated at St. Jerome's Church, at Mapusa. Known to Catholics as Our Lady of Miracles, she is also revered by Hindus who believe her to be the sister of the Hindu goddess Lairai, the presiding deity in the nearby village of Shirgao. In fact, legend has it that *Milagris Saibin* as she is known, was one of the seven goddess sisters of Hindu mythology who was converted to Christianity by the Portuguese. There are several other examples of this kind of overlapping of traditional beliefs celebrated harmoniously by both communities. On the feast day, both Catholics and Hindus flock to the church with their offerings of either candles or of oil.

The Shirgao *zatra* of the Hindu goddess Lairai, considered to be the younger sibling of *Milagris Saibin*, is celebrated within a few days of the Milagres feast. Thousands of people gather from afar for this festival, with religious rituals beginning from early morning. According to ancient legend, the village of Shirgao was once set afire by demons wishing to destroy the goddess Lairai. However, she and her devotees walked through the flames and extinguished them. Today, the highlight of the *zatra* takes place when scores of devotees commemorate this event by walking barefoot across burning live embers of red-hot coal after days of prayer and meditation.

Id-ul-Zuha, also known as Bakri Id, is a Muslim festival that commemorates an event when the Prophet Ibrahim was tested by Allah to prove his faith. Asked to sacrifice his son, Ibrahim blind-folded himself and made the offering as requested. When he removed the blindfold and opened his eyes, he was amazed and relieved to find his son alive and well, and a ram lying instead on the sacrificial altar. Since then the event is celebrated with joyous festivity.

The feast of the Holy Spirit is celebrated with much grandeur in Margao just before the onset of the monsoons. Consequently, apart from the usual items on sale, the fair here sees a veritable display of all kinds of provisions like dry fish, onions, pickles and dry chillies, thus allowing people to stock up for the long rainy days ahead.

On 24th June is the Feast of São Joao or St. John the Baptist, a festival said to commemorate the event when John the Baptist leaped for joy in his mother's womb. On this day,

to the accompaniment of much merriment and laughter, young men from the village, particularly the newly wed sons-in-law, don coronets of fresh leaves and flowers and then leap into brimming wells. The festivities are all the more riotous as participants often imbibe small amounts of *feni* before taking the customary plunge accompanied by chants of "São Joao, São Joao!"

Sangodd, a festival of the fishing community, celebrated a few days later is another example of communal amity as fishermen from both the Catholic and Hindu communities participate in the festivities. This festival is celebrated with much fervour in the Bardez Taluka. The celebrations commence with religious rituals. Later, gaily decorated boats tied together form makeshift stages where folk dances and musical programs are performed before the appreciative audience watching from the banks of the river.

The origin of the Saptah festival, celebrated at Vasco three days after Nag Panchami, is interesting. More than a century ago, the town of Vasco was ravaged by a terrible disease that saw its residents dying in large numbers. With no cure in sight, panicky citizens travelled to the temple at Zambaulim

to invoke the blessings of Lord Damodar. Soon after, the epidemic ceased and till today grateful residents celebrate at a temple of Lord Damodar set up in their town. Celebrations here take place on a grand scale with a massive fair that lasts for over a week.

Bonderam, the harvest festival celebrated on the island of Divar, has a fascinating history. The story goes that due to frequent disputes between different wards in the village, a demarcation of boundaries using flags was introduced. Rival groups, however, knocked down the demarcation flags, leading to fights between the bickering factions. The Bonderam festival is celebrated in commemoration of those long-ago events. Until recently, mock fights were also staged using toy weapons made out of bamboo stems with berries as the ammunition. Today, colourful flag marches are performed and the parades are a delight to witness.

Then comes Ganesh Chaturthi, the popular festival of the much-beloved elephant-headed God, a time when most Hindus return to ancestral homes to celebrate this joyous occasion together. The *matolli* (canopy) where the idol is placed is decorated with brightly coloured vegetables, fruits and berries. It is a time for delicious *modaks* and *ladoos* and all kinds of festive fare. The festival culminates with the immersion of the Ganesh idol to the sound of enthusiastic chants, "*Ganpati bappa morya, fuldea varsha laukar ya*" and the euphoria slowly fades till the next year.

Diwali, known popularly as the Festival of Lights, is celebrated in Goa as in other parts of the country. A day earlier, huge effigies of the demon Narkasur are made which are then burned at sunrise. Many towns have late-night Narkasur

competitions and the huge effigies, with bulging muscles and protruding tongues, are worth seeing. On the occasion of Diwali, gaily decorated and brightly lit lanterns adorn homes, the traditional Lakshmi *puja* is performed at business establishments and children delight in fireworks and sparklers of all kinds. Another local festival celebrated at this time is the boat festival at Sanquelim, which traces its origins to ancient times when lamps were set afloat on the sacred Valvanti River to mark the end of the Diwali festivities. Traditional clay lamps used in those days slowly gave way to lamps and lamp holders of different materials like bamboo, paper and banana leaves. Nowadays, boats made of various materials are illuminated and set afloat, creating a dazzling blaze of light that brightens the night and reflects on the rippling waters of the river.

Christmas marks the birth of Jesus Christ, and with New Year just around the corner, the festive spirit is evident

everywhere. Homes are decorated with illuminated stars, cribs depict the nativity scene, and Christmas trees are festooned with brightly coloured baubles, twinkling lights and sparkling tinsel. Midnight Masses are held in most churches. Children especially enjoy the festival with traditional sweets and stockings that overflow with gifts from Santa Claus. Finally, the New Year is ushered in with much enthusiasm, partying and revelry.

A very quaint custom is observed on the feast day of St. Anne at St. Anne's Church at Santana, Telaulim, where people of all faiths come to ask for particular favours. The saint is believed to be extremely generous, especially in bestowing specific favours like granting children to the childless and spouses to the single. For this, offerings of cucumbers, *urid* (pulses) or spoons are made according to the nature of one's request while reciting a charmingly appropriate rhyme in Portuguese.

A couple eager for a child will offer a cucumber (*pepino*) and ask for a baby (*menino*) saying, "*Toma este pepino e dei-me menino.*"

Unmarried maidens offer *urid* asking for a *marido* (husband) while reciting, "*Toma este urido e dei-me marido.*"

Young men offer a spoon (*colher*) and ask for a wife (*mulher*) saying, "*Toma esta colher e dei-me mulher.*"

Indeed, with so many people flocking here with their offerings, this feast is commonly known as '*Tousheachem Fest*' or Feast of Cucumbers!

Call Of The Wild

     With so many beautiful yet diverse landscapes, Goa never ceases to fascinate. Apart from the lovely golden beaches, Goa has other natural bounties that are equally as enticing. Cool forested interiors coupled with large areas of emerald green countryside, offer the perfect opportunity to experience a peaceful and refreshing rendezvous with nature. And as you trek along the winding trails in the lush forests, you cannot fail to be fascinated by the immense variety of natural wildlife. Catching a glimpse of a herd of bison, admiring a tiny tree frog poised on a green leaf or even just relaxing amidst the chorus of melodious birdsong, can be a very rewarding and enriching experience indeed. Best of all, one need not travel very far to take a walk on Goa's wild side. About 755 sq. kilometres of land, which make up almost one-fifth of Goa's total land area of 3,702 sq. kilometres, has been declared as wildlife protected area. These rich forest reserves, ranging from evergreen to moist deciduous, are home to a stunning array of flora and fauna and most of them lie along the Western Ghats, a well-known ecological hotspot of bio-diversity.

Above: A couple of Spotted Deer foraging in the grass at mollem.

Facing page: Leopards are occasionally spotted in parts of rural Goa, but are today fighting an increasingly difficult battle for survival.

Wildlife Sanctuaries

Goa presently has five wildlife sanctuaries and one National Park, all maintained by the Goa Government's Forest Department. The sanctuaries are the Bhagwan Mahavir Wildlife Sanctuary, the Bondla Wildlife Sanctuary, the Cotigao Wildlife Sanctuary, the Mhadei Wildlife Sanctuary and the Netravali Wildlife Sanctuary. The Mollem National Park lies within the core area of the Bhagwan Mahavir Wildlife Sanctuary giving it the advantage of enhanced protection befitting the status of a national park. If you'd like to spend a longer time communing with nature, accommodation is available at or close to the sanctuaries at Bondla, Mollem and Cotigao, though not as yet at the more recently notified Mhadei and Netravali sanctuaries. The accommodation at the sanctuaries is comfortable but unpretentious, making your stay more of a back-to-nature retreat. The best time to visit any of these sanctuaries is just after the monsoons, when the whole area is lush green and the waterholes are full. Clamber up to the watchtowers nearby where you may be able to catch a glimpse of the animals that come to drink there. The air is fresh and crisp and though you may require a little patience and time to spot the larger wildlife, you are sure to encounter a fascinating variety of flora and fauna.

The Bhagwan Mahavir Wildlife Sanctuary and the Mollem National Park are located at Mollem in the Sanguem Taluka, close to Goa's eastern border with Karnataka. Together they cover an area of about 240 sq. km. and are home to a wide variety of wildlife like the sloth bear, bison, deer, panthers, wild boar, the leopard cat, jungle cat, porcupines, giant spiders, the flying lizard and many species of snakes and birds. Trek along winding mud trails where the only sounds you hear are those of the jungle. Bird calls echo through the forest and as you listen to a Malabar Whistling Thrush burst into its cheeky, irrepressible melody, you understand just why the bird is also known as 'the whistling schoolboy'! Monkeys frolic in the trees overhead, and the gurgle of small streams flowing over smooth pebbles is soothing. Walk up to the Sunset Point for a glorious view of the sun as it slowly sinks below the horizon amidst a blaze of red-and-gold brilliance. Not too far from there is the Dudhsagar waterfall (aptly named, as *dudhsagar* means 'sea of milk'), about 18 kilometres from the main gate at Mollem, an ideal destination for the adventurous trekker. Closer to the falls, panoramic views of the valley below are breathtaking. The sight of Dudhsagar's milky-white waters, cascading down hundreds of metres in a powerful frothy deluge over huge black boulders, is awesome and the spot is truly worth a visit, especially just after the monsoons when the falls are in full flow. Jeeps also ply to the falls from the nearby Collem Railway Station.

The Bondla Sanctuary with a total area of just 7.98 sq. kilometres, is located near Usgao at the junction of the Ponda, Sanguem and Sattari Talukas. With its beautiful, well-tended botanical and formal gardens, this sanctuary usually attracts a lot of visitors. There is also a mini zoo (closed on Thursdays, though) where you can see porcupines, wild boar, panthers, sloth bear, peacocks, jackals, *gaur* (Indian bison), etc. Gaze in fascination as a King Cobra slithers through the vegetation in the snake pit or watch the crocodiles in their enclosure as they clamber out of the water to lazily sun themselves on the rocks close by. Alternatively, you can wander along nature trails, admiring pretty butterflies like the Blue Pansy, the Crimson Rose, the attractive Commander and scores of others as they gaily flutter along. Deer can be spotted here, and this is an excellent place for bird watching as well. Birds that have been seen here include the Oriental dwarf kingfisher, the heart-spotted woodpecker, the ruby-throated yellow bulbul, Indian Scimitar babbler and the brown fish owl.

The Cotigao Wildlife Sanctuary is located in the Canacona Taluka and occupies a total area of 85.65 sq. kilometres of dense forest. Tall trees, mostly of the moist deciduous variety, are found here as well as a wealth of flora and fauna. Hike along mud trails where you might come across pug marks of various animals, exotic species of wild plants, large termite hills, or maybe even a few discarded porcupine quills. The animals spotted here include the black panther, hyena, pangolin, giant red Malabar squirrel, sloth bear, slender loris and many varieties of deer like the mouse deer, spotted deer and barking deer. As in the other sanctuaries, there is a great abundance of bird life here as well. There are a number of watchtowers too, the most interesting one being an 18-metre high, comfortable shelter atop a tree, which affords a breathtaking view of a nearby waterhole and the surrounding lush forest.

Sacred Groves

Sacred groves are patches of pristine forest area where right from ancient times traditional worship of local deities, forest spirits, plants or animals was carried out. Cutting of plants or harming of any form of life within this protected area was strictly forbidden. The groves are thus a very significant part of Goa's ecological heritage. The concept of the groves was probably a traditional method adopted by ancestors to conserve the rich bio-diversity of the forests. Consequently, each grove remained in a near-natural state and was a haven for many rare species of birds, insects, snakes, smaller wildlife and also many medicinal plants. With their pristine, thickly wooded vegetation, the groves can be easily distinguished from other areas in the forest where there has been human interference. Most groves are located near water bodies such as springs or streams where they prevent soil erosion and help in conservation of water, thus augmenting the

water reserves of nearby communities. Rajendra Kerkar, an ardent environmentalist from Keri, Sattari, who has extensively studied various aspects of the groves in Goa says, "Sacred groves are the best example of the way in which the community has, for generations together, not only conserved forests but also wildlife. These groves are verdant green patches comparable to an oasis in the desert and constitute a unique example of the in-situ conservation of the genetic bio-diversity of our flora and fauna. They

are also extremely important in terms of conserving and providing water for drinking and irrigation. Even in this day and age, we have examples of sacred groves where not a leaf has been removed for hundreds of years. The sacred groves thus serve as valuable storehouses of age-old, untouched pristine bio-diversity."

Due to commercial interests, increasing urbanization and a weakening of traditional beliefs, the sacred groves have slowly dwindled in number. Fortunately, some still remain in the interior areas of Valpoi, Sattari, Pernem, Bicholim, Sanguem, Quepem and Canacona. The largest sacred grove in Goa is the *Ajobachi Rai*, spread over an area of about 10 hectares and located in the village of Keri, Sattari. The villagers here worship a holy spirit called '*Ajoba*' (grandfather). There is a small shrine at a nearby temple where devotees of all religions still make traditional offerings in the form of cock and goat sacrifices. Other groves in the Valpoi and Sattari areas of North Goa include *Nirankarichi Rai*, *Ghotgachi Rai* and the Kopardem Sacred Grove. *Nirankarichi Rai* is somewhat small, comprising an area of just 0.25 hectares. The god 'Nirankar'

is the reigning deity of this grove and is also considered the protector of the three nearby villages of Maloli, Ustem and Nanodem. A distinctive feature of the trees here is that their aerial roots are seen bent over the surface of the soil in an inverted 'U' shape. The Kopardem grove located in Kopardem village at Valpoi Thane has several ancient icons of different deities. Some are housed in a small shrine near the grove, while many can be seen within the grove itself. These include icons of Bhudevi, Brahmani Maya and Gajalaxmi as well as of warrior gods and other deities. An eerie glow is apparently visible in this grove on moonlit nights, which is said to be due to an unusual luminescence of fungus. Sacred groves are considered as hallowed areas, and when visiting the groves, one should abide by traditional conventions like removing footwear and not disturbing any life forms.

Birdwatching

Goa's entire countryside, especially the wooded locales and the areas around lakes and springs, are home to several species of birds. For the avid birdwatcher though, the Dr. Salim Ali

tailed jacanas, red-rumped swallows, etc. There are also private resorts (like Wildernest in the Chorlem *ghats* and Backwoods near Mollem) which offer refreshing nature getaways in the company of experienced guides.

Turtle Nesting

The famed Olive Ridley turtles visit Goa's shores every year during the months from November to March in order to lay their eggs. Earlier endangered by illegal hunting, the past few years have seen major awareness and conservation efforts that have proved highly successful in protecting the species. Olive Ridley turtles are now returning in increasing numbers to the beaches of Morjim in North Goa and Galgibag and Agonda in South Goa for nesting. In a welcome turn-around, the villagers who used to earlier hunt the turtles for their eggs and meat are now actively involved in their protection. During the nesting season, lots of onlookers gather to watch the awesome sight of baby hatchlings as they emerge from their nests on the shore and head for the sea.

Bird Sanctuary located on the island of Chorao, about 5 kilometres from Panjim, is an ornithologist's delight. Maintained by the Goa Government's Forest Department, this sanctuary comprises large areas of mangroves criss-crossed by water canals. Tiny marine life like plankton shrimps and crabs breed amongst the stilt roots of the different species of mangroves, and provide a rich feeding ground to the hundreds of birds that flock to the sanctuary. You can hire a private canoe on the island and cruise along the canals, feasting your eyes upon the rich variety of bird life around. There are resident birds like drongos, purple sunbirds, weaverbirds, sandpipers, little green herons, egrets, eagles as well as migratory birds like cormorants, storks, terns, mallard and pintail ducks that flock there between November to February. There is other wildlife here as well, and you may just be lucky enough to spot a couple of sleek otter pups frolicking in the waters.

The Carambolim Lake near the Karmali Railway Station about 12 kilometres from Panjim is also well worth a visit after the monsoon rains are over. Once the water levels recede, birds flock here in the hundreds. The marshy land hosts a variety of birdlife including the purple moorhen, white-tailed lapwings, barbets, bronze-winged and pheasant

Above: A kingfisher perched prettily, in the salim Ali Bird Sanctuary at Chorao.

Top: A lonesome egret at Dr. Salim Ali Bird Sanctuary.

Facing page: The marshy land towards hosts a variety of bird life, where birds flock in the hundreds.

Time to bid Goodbye...

Goa means many things to many people and if you've been lucky enough to have had the chance to absorb the myriad experiences that this land has to offer, you will undoubtedly find that you have been enriched by all that you have seen and done. Beautiful landscapes, a rich cultural heritage and the friendliness of its people all add up to the singular charm that is Goa. But finally, the time arrives when you have to bid goodbye, or as one would say in Konkani, 'adeus korcho vell paulo.' And whether native Goan or a visitor, it is almost certain that there will be a tinge of regret when it is time to leave. But as you remember the times you've spent here, perhaps when a sudden flood of happy memories tumbles in or when you unexpectedly catch yourself humming the seductive melody of 'Aum saiba poltodi vetam,' realization will dawn that however far you may travel, those cherished memories of Goa will always remain with you – a little bit of this beautiful land etched forever in your heart. And it's a thought that will surely bring a smile onto your lips as you whisper 'Adeus.'